on track ...

Aphex Twin

every album, every song

Beau Waddell

D0767887

sonicbondpublishing.com

Sonicbond Publishing Limited
www.sonicbondpublishing.co.uk
Email: info@sonicbondpublishing.co.uk

First Published in the United Kingdom 2023
First Published in the United States 2023

British Library Cataloguing in Publication Data:
A Catalogue record for this book is available from the British Library

Copyright Beau Waddell 2023

ISBN 978-1-78952-267-9

Typeset in ITC Garamond & ITC Avant Garde
Printed and bound in England

Graphic design and typesetting: Full Moon Media

Follow us on social media:
Twitter: https://twitter.com/SonicbondP
Instagram: https://www.instagram.com/sonicbondpublishing_/
Facebook: https://www.facebook.com/SonicbondPublishing/

Linktree QR code:

on track ... Aphex Twin

Contents

Acknowledgements

For my family

..and thanks to Sadie for taking
my picture for the back cover

Introduction and Biography

The word 'genius' seems to get tossed about every which way when you're talking about music, and more often than not – within the subjective criteria we set for ourselves – it seems justified. If we look at the dictionary definition, it says that to be a genius, a person needs to have 'exceptional skill in a particular area of activity'. In that case, what do we call Richard D. James AKA Aphex Twin (AKA Polygon Window, Caustic Window, The Tuss... the list goes on)? It's extremely rare to find an artist with so much of what seems to be effortless talent in so many different musical 'area(s) of activity'. It's even more rare to find one that can run the gamut from brushing against pop stardom to releasing projects that the wider world wouldn't even realise were masterminded by him.

James' musical adventures date back to 1985 when he was 14 (according to him at least: a deliberately vague and unreliable source at best) and – according to David Stubbs' book *Mars by 1980* – James' sister's constant playing of 'bloody awful' Jesus and Mary Chain records. James then created tracks under the pseudonym Phonic Boy on Dope: the first of many unique aliases. He took pride in dismantling synthesizers and building his own instruments through knowledge assimilated from his Cornwall College diploma in engineering. Once he felt he'd gained enough experience – either from purchasing as many techno and house records as he could, or from playing fledgling DJ sets where he secretly dropped-in many of his own early tracks – James became involved in the Cornwall 'free party' scene. These were raves that took place in hidden coves, dunes or even barns: whatever prevented the police from shutting them down.

Soon he began a DJ residency at the Crantock Bowgie club, where – as detailed in the *Analogue Bubblebath 1* and *2* entries – he was persuaded to release his demo tapes on Mark Darby's Mighty Force record label. James also met future Rephlex partner Grant Wilson-Claridge at the club. These EPs helped bolster James' underground following, contributing to his success at his next record label R&S, when the *Digeridoo* EP reached 55 in the UK singles chart. The same box of tapes that James and R&S owner Renaat Vondepapaliere sourced the *Digeridoo* tracks from, held the material that later became the groundbreaking *Selected Ambient Works 85-92* album. It's still considered a benchmark electronic music LP, generating the source code for IDM (or braindance: the term James prefers) and ambient techno in its 13 tracks.

Over the next two years, a virtual minefield of creativity burst open, with James simultaneously releasing projects under three or four different aliases – the debuts of Polygon Window, Caustic Window and Bradley Strider all happening in the same short period. This led to the release of the next full-length Aphex Twin album: *Selected Ambient Works Volume II*. Released on Warp Records – James' label for all his mainline projects – it's another foundation stone, this time for dark-ambient music.

This (frankly) unparalleled work ethic sustained into 1995 with the release of two deeply inspirational projects. First was the third Aphex Twin album *...I Care Because You Do*, which fused Modern Classical experimentation and some of the hardest-hitting beats of James' career (and started the trend of his artwork showing his face as grotesquely contorted). Secondly came the AFX *Hangable Auto Bulb* EPs, which tapped into the rise of drum-'n'-bass in the mainstream. James used digital workstations to edit the percussion into mind-bending patterns, to form the basis of drill-'n'-bass. James' work to perfect this physics-defying subgenre was complete with the fourth Aphex Twin LP *Richard D. James Album*, which had another nightmarish, grinning James visage on the front. The record fine-tuned the beats, repeated the classical ventures of *...ICBYD* and juxtaposed some of the sweetest melodies of James' career against scathing drum programming.

The late-1990s were capped-off with (among a multitude of side projects) James' commercial ascendancy, courtesy of what have become two of his most well-known EPs. 'Pappy Mix' – *Come to Daddy*'s mix of the title track – gave James his biggest hit since 'Digeridoo', partly due to the innovative and terrifying imagery in the Chris Cunningham-helmed video. 'Windowlicker' also came with a Cunningham promo – even more disturbing than the last – but the skewed pop sensibility wasn't lost on the public, who got the single to number 16. But unhappy with this exposure, James pulled the single: preventing it from reaching the top 10.

Two years of relative dormancy resulted in 2001's *Drukqs* – another sprawling work in the vein of *SAW Volume II*. Its ultra-fast acid-infused drill-'n'-bass provided us with the apotheosis of James' technical mastery. On the other hand, it's electroacoustic and modern-classical experiments showed another side to James' compositional style – proving he was no amateur in less-electronic genres. The rushed release of the LP – the result of James' MP3 player containing hundreds of unreleased Aphex Twin tracks being left on a plane – gave way to a long hiatus for the Aphex Twin name. That doesn't mean he was completely inactive. In fact, James found the time to release 11 EPs in his analogue synth-only *Analord* series, and also kept fans guessing with his mysterious (and at the time unconfirmed) assumption of the Tuss persona.

In 2014, giant publicity stunts teased with the first new Aphex album in 13 years in 2014 – *Syro* released later that year to a rapturous reception. Despite not being as forward-thinking as his prior LPs, it provided an opportunity to hear James honing all the skills he'd amassed in the years out of the spotlight. This revitalised interest sparked a four-year creative period, where he dabbled in more electroacoustic compositions with vintage synths, and his drum programming became increasingly complex. Amongst all this, he also uploaded hundreds of unreleased tracks to Soundcloud on an anonymous profile, which fans dubbed the Soundcloud Dump.

Producing so much varied material over such a relatively-short period of time (at least in proportion to the overall discography size) is awe-inspiring, no matter the quality. And while there are times when the compositions seem lacklustre or uninspired, it's made up for by the beauty and nostalgia so much of his other output evokes. The list of musicians inspired by James speaks for itself – whether it's Skrillex or Thom Yorke, Daft Punk or Steve Reich, James' music has touched something in them to provoke the creative process: perhaps the biggest compliment someone's art can attain.

In this book, I have done my best to track down and cover every Aphex Twin LP, EP and single, including all relevant bonus tracks that can be found on reissues or the Aphex Twin website. But there are some disclaimers:

A: If a project is made up of more than 50% remixes, it won't be covered. Hence, the absence of the *26 Mixes for Cash* remix compilation.

B: Any projects that have remained officially *unreleased* will not be discussed. For example, the *Analogue Bubblebath 5* EP. The only exception is the *Caustic Window* LP, as that was given a widespread, official digital release.

C: Some projects are left out purely for their lack of real impact on James' career, or for the murk surrounding their release officiality. For example, the *3 Gerald Remix* single.

In 2017, James uploaded most of his back catalogue to his new website, adding many bonus tracks sourced from the period of each project. There will be many instances where these tracks will appear – always discussed at the end of a particular project. Some come with notes from James himself, which I will highlight at the relevant point. They will always appear in the order they're listed on the Aphex Twin website.

With all of that out of the way, I sincerely hope you enjoy the book. Hopefully, you'll find out something new about James' music, and be persuaded to delve deeper into the discography of this peerless artist.

All of this music is by Richard D. James, except where marked.

The EPs, Part 1: 1991-1992
Analogue Bubblebath (1991)
Alias: The Aphex Twin
Personnel:
Richard D. James: Producer, all instruments
Co-producer: Schizophrenia ('Entrance To Exit')
Release date: September 1991
Chart placings: Did not chart
Running time: 19:53
Record label: Mighty Force

Despite allegedly making music since the age of 14 in 1985, it wasn't until 1991 that James finally formally released his work. He was initially reluctant to release anything, being more content with producing cassettes for friends or playing in Newquay's Bowgie club for a handful of individuals. It was only the intervention of Mark Darby – creator of the Mighty Force record label – that persuaded James to distribute his cassettes to a larger audience, after performing at a Plymouth Academy rave. Darby told *Record Collector* in 2018: 'I think it was because he was really tripped out and he just wanted us to fuck off, so he said, 'Yes'. I think if he had not done that trip that night, there may have never been any Aphex Twin'.

The record in question was a C90 tape that eventually became James' first official release *Analogue Bubblebath*. This began not only a series of sequel EPs but became the source for many future Aphex Twin tracks.

'Analogue Bubblebath' (4:40)
This agreeable slice of bubbly chill-out techno contrasts heavily with the rest of the EP. A simple electronic drum loop (a world away from the percussive technicality that became one of James' hallmarks later in his career) is surrounded by an ever-present synth drone, to which some Orbital-esque staccato chords are added. After a brief breakdown, the piece coalesces and sees itself out with a disjunct synth melody and a false ending. Altogether, it's a pleasant-enough premiere to the world of Aphex Twin, doesn't feel fully formed enough to warrant its sometime status as a classic.

'Isoprophlex' ('Isopropophlex' on the original issue) (5:19)
The first example of the many mind-numbing, repetitive acid-techno pieces James released in the first two years. As with the others, this is a fairly uneventful track, only distinguished by its dreamy truncated sampling: allegedly of Julie Andrews from *The Sound of Music*. It was replicated in an extended version on the vinyl *Digeridoo* EP.

'Entrance to Exit' (Co-produced by Schizophrenia) (4:22)
This collaboration sustains the previous track's industrial undertones, the grimy bass accented by samples of metal being hit – perhaps a nod to

Kraftwerk's groundbreaking 'Metal On Metal', which utilised metallic sounds as a percussive base. Sadly, this piece isn't nearly as innovative as that example, leaving a lot to be desired in its incessant wailing and pounding – only recommended over 'Isoprophlex' due to its greater audio intensity.

'AFX 2' (5:26)

Another distorted drumbeat ushers in the EP closer, paired with atonal, electronic bursts that prefigure 'Ventolin' from 1995's *...I Care Because You Do*. This is then jettisoned for a groovier middle that introduces spooky keyboard motifs and a trance bass line that's still overshadowed by the overdriven drums, causing the few different ideas to be lost in the mix.

Analogue Bubblebath 2 (1991)
Alias: Aphex Twin
Personnel:
Richard D. James: Producer, all instruments
Release date: December 1991
Chart placings: Did not chart
Running time: 14:53
Record label: Rabbit City Records

This EP was James' first release under solely 'Aphex Twin' rather than AFX or The Aphex Twin. The first side consists of 'Digeridoo', but was listed under a different name, as James had two record deals at the time. Rabbit City Records released this EP quickly, with no cover art and only a white label displaying the track list and Aphex Twin moniker. When James' other record label R&S caught wind of the fact that 'Digeridoo' (originally promised to them) was already being sold on a different release, they bought every copy they could find: making the original issue extremely rare.

'Aboriginal Mix' (7:10)
The first appearance of the well-known 'Digeridoo' before its more widespread placement on its eponymous EP. We'll talk about the track in more detail in that section.

'Untitled' (3:44)
Although this follows a similar pattern to the weakest tracks on *Analogue Bubblebath*, the distorted bass line actually offers an earworm to latch onto, with the pummelling backbeat enhanced by more-subtle sound design – especially those lovely reversed pianos. It's not fantastic, but it's a step up from the numbing rave fodder on the first EP.

'Untitled' (3:59)
Pretty much a repeat of the first untitled track, the EP closer contains another overdriven and crunchy 303 bass line, coupled with a thumping techno beat.

It's standard fare for Aphex at the time, with nothing much to make it stand out from the rest of its acid techno ilk.

Digeridoo (1992)
Alias: The Aphex Twin
Personnel:
Richard D. James: Producer, all instruments
Release date: May 1992
Chart placings: UK: 55
Running Time: 25:45 (Vinyl); 24:22 (CD)
Record label: R&S

This EP is the moment James made his first true impact on the music world. Not only was it his first charting release – flying to 55 on the UK singles chart – but it garnered him his biggest press attention and praise thus far. Released at the height of the UK's obsession with rave culture (both positive and negative), the combination of a breakneck tempo and distorted minimalism made it a hit at these illicit gatherings. In a 1992 *Melody Maker* feature, Andrew Smith recounted: 'The title track is already a rave staple – wild end-of-evening techno which takes its name from the fact that punters used to chant for it (identifying with its digeridoo-like bass line) during the Aphex set'.

This was the first example of James' innovation in the rave scene, with the title track's 155 bpm pushing acid techno into more extreme and abrasive territory, away from the utopian visions of the earlier squelchy acid house singles, into something darker – a premonition of the musical juxtapositions present throughout James' career.

Also of note are the different tracklists between the vinyl and CD issues.

Vinyl: 'Digeridoo', 'Flaphead', 'Phloam', 'Isoprophlex (AKA Isopropanol)'
CD: 'Digeridoo', 'Analogue Bubblebath', 'Flaphead', 'Phloam'

'Isoprophlex' and 'Analogue Bubblebath' are essentially carbon copies of their original versions, only distinguished by small alterations in their length – so they won't be discussed again. Similarly, 'Flaphead' and 'Phloem' will only be examined once each.

'Digeridoo' (7:11)
As the first major achievement in the Aphex Twin discography, this track's main selling point is the foreboding digeridoo synth that's omniscient throughout. This was not a sample, as Simon Reynolds discussed in his book *Energy Flash: A Journey Through Dance and Rave Culture*: '(James) laboured for three days to concoct an electronic simulacrum of the primordial drone'.

Its mesh with the skittering rhythm section – not to mention the scathing tempo – is a unique reconstruction of the acid techno tropes that even *James* was embracing on past EPs. Furthermore, the subtle oscillations of the 303 synth, and flanging of the treble-heavy drumbeat, keep the track engaging through its seven minutes, capturing a delicate balance between dread and euphoria: somewhat of an Aphex speciality, as we'll see later. It's a great track – worthy of the praise it was given at the time of release.

'Flaphead' (6:41; 7:00 on the CD)
Sadly, this track doesn't continue the exciting momentum of the title track. Like many of James' earliest-released creations, it's an intermittently engaging piece of acid-infused techno. Its selling point is a glitchy, drumless section at the halfway mark, that breaks the track down into its most creative elements. That it runs for almost seven minutes doesn't improve its construction at all, unfortunately.

'Phloam' (5:33)
Another track that aligns almost exactly to James' early formula. Distorted acid squelches and bass thrums dart across the mix, alongside relentless 16th-note kick drums. The simple, vaporous three-note melody that gives colour from the 1:40 mark gives some much-needed variety away from the cut-glass mush of the other instruments.

Xylem Tube (1992)
Alias: Aphex Twin
Personnel:
Richard D. James: Producer, all instruments
Release date: June 1992
Chart placings: Did not chart
Running time: 22:03
Record label: R&S

James capitalised on the warm reception and success of *Digeridoo* by releasing another EP one month later. This project experimented more with breakbeat and more complex instrumentation but also retained many of the prior characteristics. The EP also gave us our first look at the now-iconic Aphex Twin logo, designed by Paul Nicholson. According to an Instagram post-Nicholson made in 2017: 'The original Aphex Twin logo was drawn by hand, using circle templates and rulers, in late-1991'.

'Polynomial-C' (4:44)
This is the first true representation of James' genius, and a massive improvement on the already-tired and formulaic tracks he'd been releasing. Ushered in with breathtaking arpeggios anchored by synth chord stabs, it kicks into high gear with the layering of a euphoric breakbeat: another first for James.

The composition demonstrates his acknowledgement of the importance of space, with moments of respite offered by focussing on the arpeggiator's burbling majesty. This makes the inevitable return of the breakbeat even more powerful and genuinely exciting, proving that a track can be hard-hitting, even in the absence of constant aural assault. It's a melodic landmark in James' earliest creations.

'Tamphex (Headphuq Mix)' (6:29)
Annoyingly, the EP quickly descends back into the repetition of standard hardcore acid-techno influences. Mirroring *Analogue Bubblebath*'s 'Isoprophlex' in more than just name, the implementation of creepy sampling (this time from a tampon advert) intertwined with the untamed squalls of the 303, are just too similar (yet somehow more grading) to its spiritual predecessor, to make this worthwhile.

'Phlange Phace' (5:22)
Slightly better than 'Tamphex', this number still manages to accomplish the minimum in its five and a half minutes. The reverb-heavy portent of the main melody somewhat hints at the direction taken on *Selected Ambient Works, Vol. 2.* Aside from this, it's just one more forgettable piece to add to the ever-growing list.

'Dodeccaheedron' (5:48)
This is barely indistinguishable from 'Phlange Phace', with their ominous melodic elements seemingly identical to one another. The percussion takes even more of a central role here, but that isn't enough to elevate it above its acid techno brethren.

Album: Selected Ambient Works 85-92 (1992)

Alias: Aphex Twin

Personnel:

Richard D. James: Producer, electronics, sampler

Release date: November 1992

Chart placings: UK: 10 (Dance chart) (Charted in 2014 after the release of Syro)

Running time: 74:20

Record label: Apollo

During the press promotion undertaken to spread the word about the underground success of *Digeridoo*, James revealed to *Melody Maker*'s Andrew Smith that he was working on an ambient album. Allegedly, some of the pieces were created as far back as 1985, when James was 14. (As we'll learn, these fantastic myths perpetuated by James, need to be taken with a few pinches of salt.) But if this was true, the pieces eventually released as this album (which henceforth will be abbreviated to *SAW 85-92*), take on an even-greater sense of the revolutionary achievement they already possessed in spades.

This album's influence is almost incalculable now; its pioneering fusion of techno, house and electronica forming the basis for IDM (Intelligent Dance Music – a condescending moniker that seems to forget the influence of (apparently) non-intelligent dance music on the style; not least on James himself). The abrasive relentlessness of the early EPs is eschewed for a more-subtle direction showing James' creative and innovative tendencies at their fullest potential for the first time: at least, in such a concentrated and consistent form.

Despite the 'ambient' tag, this album wears it proudly. It's a different type of ambience to Brian Eno's seminal 1970s work or John Cage's experiments with silence. It's even far-removed from its successor, *Selected Ambient Works, Volume II*. In fact, this album works as a post-rave balm, retaining many of the characteristics of the minimal techno and deep house tracks surfacing at the time, but transporting their consistent pulses into a more clear-minded atmosphere. But as with any Aphex project, there's plenty of darkness in the grooves. The latter is intertwined with James' juggling of different genres – as Jon Savage summarised beautifully in a 1993 *Village Voice* feature: '(The album) trashed the boundaries between acid, techno, ambient and psychedelic'.

As any *classic* album should, this record still manages to hold its own today amongst the multitude of artists and producers it inspired. It's a testament to its far-reaching quality that artists as disparate as Radiohead (who wore the IDM influence very plainly for the their *Kid A/Amnesiac* duology) and Boards of Canada (who have made numerous classic albums and EPs) can share a love of this LP. It's a true masterwork, and yet, is only the preface for a career packed full of them.

'Xtal' (4:51)

It's difficult to think of a better way to open an album than this: one of James' most praiseworthy creations. It sets the template for the entire album, decorated with cavernous reverb and a tentative beauty in its mixture of heavenly vocals and airy synth pads. But there is an amateurish nature to the production – the track was one example purportedly written by James when he was 14 – which embellishes the fragile interplay between the soft drum loop and the percolating digital stabs. It seems to have been recorded in another world – somewhere alternately mysterious and beatific, capturing a feeling of melancholy that betrays inherent warmth, even in an alien environment. .

'Tha' (9:01)

'Tha' is a masterpiece in sound design. James manages to conjure up the muffled, distant sound of standing outside a club, pairing fleeting glimpses of vocals with hints of a constant pulse and the meandering automation of the bass line and main synth melody. The omnipresent cloud of reverb, returns – compounding the nocturnal loneliness the decaying ambience layered on top points towards.

Unlike the long-winded tracks filling the earlier EPs, this track's nine-minute length is barely noticeable – the hypnotic cascade of sound and texture painting an alternately bleak, bizarre and inviting portrait of late-night life surrounded by technology.

'Pulsewidth' (3:47)

This track's bouncy beat and heavily-delayed, rapturous melody present the flipside to the dark desolation of 'Tha' – almost as if we're getting a glimpse inside the club we were previously outside of. On the surface, it's one of the simplest pieces here, and the least-worthy of the 'ambient' tag. However, delving deeper rewards you with a surprisingly complex web of bass and drums. Filling in each other's gaps, their isolated appearance near the end seems to indicate the stripping away of the initial joy for something more pensive.

'Ageispolis' (5:21)

This track title indicates a futuristic bent, harkening back to the utopian visions of early electronica: most likely, Kraftwerk's pulsating 'Metropolis' from 1978. The clipped, earworm of an introduction has a pentatonic quality that hints at the technological advancement of Japanese music, before a reversed haze of synths continue the journey. The best part is the subtle distortion, changes in the drums, and the sub-bass punch, making the track more of a physical experience.

'i' (1:13)

Perhaps the only track here that could be labelled as conventional ambient music, this short interlude provides a much-needed split between the record's two halves. The brief wash of synth tones acts as a pleasant palate cleanser before the album's groovier, longer section.

'Green Calx' (6:02)

The first in the 'Calx' series, this is a wild voyage into the unknown – ironically, through many elements from the past. The initial, gorgeous melody could've been easily extracted from an early OMD record, save for the characteristic acid burbles beneath it. But after this period of safety, all bets are off, as we head into a cacophony of gunfire, arcade start-ups and comic sound effects. Surprisingly, it's one of the least loved *SAW 85-92* pieces! It's preposterous – to me at least – that anyone could dislike the nestled groove the track finally settles into, especially when that introductory hook returns to see the track off.

'Heliosphan' (4:51)

Another high watermark (of which the album seems to have an infinite amount), this track's near-symphonic chord progression is masterful – enhanced by the spiritual, ghostly refrain that weaves in and out of the breakbeat. The cymbal editing here – allowing them to glitch and slur between beats – is notable for being the first glimpse of the virtuosic approach to beatmaking that James went on to have in his late-1990s work. It magnifies the track's sheer thrill, propelling it straight into the future before any others have had time to catch up. There's a sense of foreboding mystery dripping from the instrumental palette, like a quick, crystalline glimpse into another world.

'We Are The Music Makers' (7:42)

The Gene Wilder line/sample that gives this track its title, could also be a manifesto for Aphex's compositional goals at the time. Each piece's hyperreal qualities serve to *dream* of the shape of electronic music to come, with James as its pioneer the *dreamer*. Every element of the piece is unified – bass trading motifs with the melodic organ-like synths, culminating in an unparalleled groove that actively forces you to move along with it. The harmonies formed by the high-pitched keys just underline even further the importance of synergy in the music, and the beauty that can come as a result.

'Schottkey 7th Path' (5:07)

A stereotypical sci-fi-sounding melody dominates this strange track, which along with 'Hedphelym', provides the greatest link to the early AFX/The Aphex Twin projects. This mainly stems from the lone kick drum. But in this context, it's little more than an echo, fading in and out as naturally as the other instruments. The rhythm of the percussion presents a contrast in its repetition, creating a strange fusion of old and new styles as another act of recontextualising.

'Ptolemy' (7:12)

Given that the title was the name of an Egyptian mathematician, this track is suitably exotic (in the cliché sense) – most apparent in the shape-shifting, breathy sound that takes hold of the track's direction. The handclap-heavy drum part nods to the pioneers of Detroit house and techno. James cleverly fuses this with the ambient waves of sound hinted at throughout, melding abandonment (connoted by the danceable elements) and the foreboding entrance of these calmer timbres.

'Hedphelym' (6:02)

This is probably the weakest track here, but by no means bad or even middling, due to its close ties to the less-ambitious *Analogue Bubblebath* era, placing the thumping kick drum at the forefront above the multitude of ambient wails clawing underneath. The latter is the most interesting aspect – a wall of sound that's deliberately cold and uninviting; much closer to the dark ambient spearheaded by black-metal bands like Burzum than any of the new-age muzak that was creeping into the genre.

'Delphium' (5:36)

Definitely one of the most underrated Aphex tracks, this is built entirely on an addictive groove, possessed by an infectious ascending-and-descending deep-house bass line. It's embellished by trails of arpeggios that gradually become more-prevalent until they're the backbone of the entire piece – exhibited fully in a mesmerising middle section where the ambient synths drop out to leave the bond between the drums and arpeggiators in full view. It's a final burst of euphoric energy before the album winds down.

'Actium' (7:35)

The final track ends the album at the same quality level as the opener 'Xtal'. The track title is a successor to 'Delphium' and 'Hedphelym', but musically returns to the spacious sound of 'Tha'. Another delicate melody hangs over the cavernous reverb set off by the hissing drums and impressionistic bass line. The skeletal construction acts as a clear reminder of the musical distance travelled from an unsubtle track like 'Tamphex' to here. Now, the music ends in a perfect interweaving harmony, transporting us back to that strange, nocturnal environment, to close on an intriguing unresolved note.

The EPs, Part 2: 1992-1993
Joyrex J4 and J5 (1992)
Alias: Caustic Window (Both EPs)
Personnel: (Both EPs)
Richard D. James: Producer, all instruments
Release date: July 1992
Chart placings: Did not chart
Running time: 18:53 (Joyrex J4); 21:06 (Joyrex J5)
Record label: Rephlex Records

The labels of this pair of releases displayed only the basic information. No track titles were given until the later *Compilation* which collected most of the songs from these projects and their namesake follow-ups. *J4* has the distinction of having one of the few Aphex Twin cover versions: an interpretation of Hot Butter's 'Popcorn'.

Joyrex J5 follows pretty much the same formula, with no track titles given. This time the labels were adorned with playing card iconography – one of the more-recognisable aspects of the Caustic Window moniker: also appearing on the labels of *Compilation*.

Joyrex J4 (1992)
'Joyrex J4' (4:27)
The title track begins with an enveloping, oscillating tone, before quickly shifting into a plucky dark riff that introduces the four-on-the-floor techno beat. The drums increase in complexity as the track moves towards a more industrial feel. There are some intriguing ideas, but nothing that memorable.

'Pop Corn' (Gershon Kingsley) (3:38)
A slight but ultimately entertaining breakbeat-infused interpretation of the instantly recognisable Hot Butter piece. The puckish hook becomes less rigid as its layered over the 'Polynomial-C' break: a classic example of James' musical sense of humour.

'AFX 114' (1:20)
This minute-long piece samples the 'Phlange Phace' drum break, repeating it with the addition of some weird oscillator glitches.

'Cordialatron' (4:43)
A true hidden gem. A lively drum groove cradles the marimba-esque ascending synth chords, as a slurring, pillowy lead improvises on top. It prefigures the beauty of the *Surfing on Sine Waves* album, layering every element into a gorgeous, minimal lattice, making it potentially his most straightforward acid house track thus far.

'Italic Eyeball' (4:24)

Another vaguely Middle Eastern melody anchors some complex drum programming (meaning we're getting closer to the intricacy James is predominantly associated with), paired with a reversed sample of Julie Andrews (harkening back to 'Isoprophlex'). They're a pleasant mix, though it's one of the weaker tracks here.

'Pigeon Street' (0:23)

This is also known as the 'Caustic Window Jingle', which aptly describes this extremely short but surprising earworm, closing the EP with a kitsch sign-off.

Joyrex J5 (1992)

'Astroblaster' (5:27)

Looks like we're back in *Digeridoo* and *Xylem Tube* territory. The gated drums hammer through a standard overdriven bass synth before some bit-crushed chimes break through at the end. It's pretty unremarkable, especially at this stage in James' career.

'On The Romance Tip' (5:04)

Thankfully, this is mainly based on a bed of lovely, thick synth pads, which must've been an influence on Moby's side project Voodoo Child. A suitably bleepy drum track gives way to a more apprehensive segment until those chords return in their full majestic quality. It's a much-needed change of pace, putting the EP back on track.

'Joyrex J5' (6:54)

The beginning low sub-bass rumble immediately recalls 'Digeridoo': annoyingly so, as this track pales in comparison. The flanged 303 pulses have a serviceable funk. The rest is mainly sound effects that attempt to fill out what're just the bare bones.

'Untitled (R2D2)' (3:42)

This is a cute chiptune piece consisting of Pac-Man (or more likely R2-D2 from *Star* Wars) sounds that morph into a commercial house breakdown, enlivened by the hip-hop-styled thud of the kick drum. Sounds redolent of Kraftwerk's 'Pocket Calculator' close this fine ending to a slightly underwhelming project.

Analogue Bubblebath Vol. 3 (1992)

Alias: AFX

Personnel:

Richard D. James: Producer, all instruments

Release date: February 1992
Running time: 32:23 (Vinyl); 54:31 (CD)
Chart placings: Did not chart
Running time: 32:23 (Vinyl); 54:31 (CD)
Record label: Rephlex Records

James was becoming ever-more prolific, releasing another EP under the
AFX name. The packaging was this EP's main draw. The vinyl version
(shorter than the 1993 CD reissue) came in a brown paper bag with a
leaflet describing places of interest in James' native Cornwall. The CD was
even more interesting, in bubble wrap (presumably an extension of the
'bubblebath' title). Unlike the vinyl, the CD had no track titles, so the bonus
tracks affixed to this issue remain untitled to this day.

As there are two different versions of the EP, the vinyl version will be
covered first, with the CD bonus tracks at the end.

'.215061' (4:16)
A blatant rewrite of 'Polynomial-C', this contains the same burbling bass line,
punctuated by similar phased staccato synth notes. It's a shame it's so similar
to another (admittedly better) track. The original still tops this, even with the
New Order-indebted higher keyboard melody.

'.000890569' (4:31)
Another track that cleaves uncomfortably close to 'Polynomial-C', in reverse
to the previous number. Here, the breakbeat is nearly identical, though the
oscillating bass is retained. A more-plucky B-section offers a little contrast.
But altogether, a combination of poor sequencing and similar motifs makes
this track less appealing than it could've been.

'0.38' (0:38)
Nothing much to say here. It's just a distorted voice sample that foreshadows
the field-recording interludes on *Drukqs*.

'0.180871' (3:45 (Left channel), 4:10 (Right channel))
This is a unique one, being essentially two songs playing at the same time –
hard-panned to the left and right. Naturally, the effect is disorienting and a
little annoying. The left is basically one repeated bleeping arpeggio, while the
right is made up mostly of voice samples. It's an admirable endeavour but not
one that pays off.

'.55278037732581' (4:18)
The barcode-like track title is more intriguing than the contents. You guessed
it: more distorted bass, more compressed drums, and vaguely industrial noise
sprinkled throughout. It's really nothing to write home about.

'.942937' (4:31)

Most of the extremely tiring elements still loom over this track. Fortunately, James decorates these now-irritating constituent parts with lush ambient waves that seem torn from a brighter alternative version of *Selected Ambient Works, Volume II*, which would work so much better isolated as an interlude, à la 'i'.

'.1993841' (5:43)

Switching back to the mode of the earliest AFX works for the umpteenth time, the bulky drum programming and subtle automated reverb are the primary feature of interest. It must've had an impression on Radiohead's Thom Yorke, as his 2006 album *The Eraser* (specifically 'Cymbal Rush') pays homage by using the same sounds as percussive focal points.

'AFX 6/b' (0:31)

Another slim interlude of heavily-distorted sound effects and drums. There's really nothing to talk about here.

CD Bonus Tracks
'(CAT 00897-AA1) (Fluted)' (4:05)

It's surprising that this was left off the original issue, as it has one of the most-twinkly melodies of any of the *Analogue Bubblebath* tracks. The naked, innocent lead is juxtaposed against ambient echoes that descend into darkness as the melodic elements disappear.

'(CAT 00897-A1)' (5:06)

The drums here are extremely up-front, making them especially nauseating: which works to the track's advantage. Samples of children laughing are interspersed into the mostly-sparse instrumentation, but nothing really meshes as it should.

'Untitled (track 11)' (4:41)

This is an extremely disturbing piece. With its lack of title, and spectral atmosphere, it feels like it precedes *Selected Ambient Works, Volume II*. The unexpected crunchy effects that burst out of the desolate pads, add to the overall horror, with heavily-processed screaming increasing the tension of the frequencies left by the ambient decays enveloping the listener.

'Untitled (track 12)' (0:53)

Rain noise and the distorted sound of heavy breathing, fill this meaningless postscript to the prior track.

'(CAT 00897-A2)' (5:14)

This is practically the same as '(CAT 00897-A1)' (presumably why their titles are related). More-lenient use of reverb and volume automation here makes the track feel larger, even though it recycles the techniques dispatched on its related piece.

Album: **Surfing on Sine Waves** (1993)
Alias: **Polygon Window**
Personnel:
Richard D. James: Producer, writing, arrangement, programming, engineering, location recording
Beau Thomas: Mastering
Release date: January 1993
Chart placings: Did not chart
Running time: 49:02 (Original version); 56:58 (Reissue); 62:34 (Website)
Record label: Warp Records

Surfing on Sine Waves is another crucial point in James' recording career, being his first full release on Warp Records – the label he'd be inextricably tied to in genre and sound for the remainder of his discography. However, this wasn't the first time he was linked with the label – in July 1992, Warp released the seminal *Artificial Intelligence* compilation, the opener of which was a track called 'Polygon Window' by a mysterious producer known only as The Dice Man. Inevitably, this turned out to be James, whose fusion of ambient, techno, house and electronica, paved the way for the IDM genre the compilation promoted.

He reused the Polygon Window name (somewhat of a sequel to Caustic Window, one would imagine) for this album, which contains many references to his native Cornwall. The cover is a picture Chapel Porth beach, where James claims he 'nearly drowned' when he was younger. The extra tracks included on the 2001 reissue pay tribute to Portreath Harbour and Redruth School – the latter being where James studied, according to a 2016 feature in *The Quietus*.

'Polygon Window' (5:24)
The second appearance of the eponymous track, it sets out the template for the more-techno-indebted pieces littering the album – clean production, a formidable bass line, melodic synth textures, and repetitive-yet-complex drum programming. On its own, it doesn't quite match the atmosphere of *SAW 85-92*, but its constantly-shifting timbres were an inspiration to many fellow 'Braindance' travellers.

'Audax Powder' (4:36)
The obvious musical distance between the idyllic synth warbles and harsh lead, is challenged throughout by their gradual layering, forming a symbiotic bond between two disparate elements. The strength of each – whether melodic or rhythmic – is showcased through sections that force the two apart, almost creating two separate compositional strands in the process.

'Quoth' (5:34)
Probably the most well-known track here besides the title song, 'Quoth' strips away the cleanliness of the earlier pieces, leaving a pulsating shell. It's the

production that stops this track from becoming monotonous – the muffled kick drum, paired with the rough percussion, conjures an atmosphere of primitive rave, acknowledging the prehistoric lineage of rhythm's importance to humanity.

'If It Really Is Me' (7:01)

The simplest piece here – at least on the surface – is actually my favourite. A pristine house piano hammers out chords, syncopated over the conveyer-belt rhythm track. A droning organ and a chiptune keyboard build on the trance-like feel by introducing tight-knit instrumental interplay. When the track bleeds into a trippy house breakdown, each integral segment slowly returns until the glorious lattice of electronics is reinstated in full. This use of tension and release clearly owes a lot to Manuel Göttsching's *E2-E4*: the guitarist's proto-electronica masterwork.

'Supremacy II' (4:04)

It's back to sinister techno business as usual, at least at first. As the track progresses – mainly following the now-standard Julie Andrews sample – the drums become closer to the stifling intensity of 'Quoth', skittering alongside the mechanical oscillations, while the off-kilter melody becomes more glitchy and fragmented.

'UT1-dot' (5:17)

This is the most anonymous piece here, mainly due to its gloopy 303 bass and menacing reverbed ostinati being able to slot easily into one of the *Analogue Bubblebath* EPs. The robotic vocals are close to the ones Kraftwerk used on their underrated 1986 LP *Electric Café*.

'(untitled)' (6:24)

Without the driving drum loop and scratchy 303, this could plausibly fit somewhere on *Selected Ambient Works, Volume II*. The track seems somewhat confused in its direction. Both major elements are interesting, though the glacial drift of the pads is the most gripping. But in this case, they don't gel very well at all.

'Quixote' (6:00)

The thicker sound palette here allows the ambient layers to be better integrated into the overall piece. The addictive bass line is much more potent than the squall of '(untitled)', and the airy synths punctuate the sharp techno beat and handclap flurries, rather than work against them.

'Quino – phec' (4:42)

A crystalline beauty to finish the record off. Like 'Quoth', the production steals the show, despite the track being the antithesis of the former's aggravation. Everything is pooled together into a haze of distant hints at percussion and melodica. The everyday ambience captured allows the music to become one with the environment it's played in, reaching a pure form of ambience that would be further explored in *SAW, Volume II*.

2001 reissue bonus tracks (In the order of album appearance)
'Portreath Harbour' (4:44)
A tightly-constructed, nostalgic entry, utilising the 'On' synth sound, months before that track was released. It eschews the techno influence that permeates the rest of the album, favouring a syncopated beat that – with the addition of creaking effects and the growing kick-drum distortion – becomes more dark and scary as it moves along.

'Redruth School' (2:43)
A more modern-classical approach leaks into this piece, with tuned percussion filling out the melodic role around the shifting beat. It's a perfect sound for James, as it conveys a sense of melody while also having a sinister microtonal quality to keep the balance intact. This track is fine enough, but James' more developed dives into this genre are yet to come.

Website bonus tracks
'clissold 101(dat28 otari) 48k' (5:43)
Originally part of the legendary Soundcloud Dump (where James released hundreds of unreleased tracks online under different aliases), this track should've been worthy of a place on the album proper. It has an enchanting melody (using that pentatonic scale again) and some advanced drums that remain locked into the groove set by the synth chimes that fade into ambient loveliness as the track progresses.

The EPs, Part 3: 1993
Quoth (1993)
Alias: Polygon Window
Personnel:
Richard D. James: Producer, writing, arrangement, programming, engineering, location recording
Release date: March 1993
Chart placings: UK: 49
Running time: 30:51
Record label: Warp Records

This second and final release under the Polygon Window name is inextricably tied to *Surfing on Sine Waves*, with 'Quoth' forming the basis of the majority of the project. Therefore, it proves to be James' most techno-focussed project, and, overall, one of his darkest-sounding. The vinyl version came on clear vinyl, and there was a black test pressing, which is quite rare. Exclusive to the CD was the 'Hidden Mix' of 'Quoth': unavailable on any other format.

Considering this release's harsh, underground (cleverly interpreted by the memorable cover) nature, it surprisingly managed to reach 50 in the UK singles chart no less.

'Iketa' (4:31)
This track could've easily fit on the second half of *Surfing on Sine Waves* – utilising a similar palette of spacious ambience, scathing 303 bass screeches and a busy drum section. Like many of the album's less-musically-ambitious pieces, the production choices (including copious reverb and magnanimous distortion) liven-up the track considerably.

'Quoth (Wooden Thump Mix)' (7:57)
The EP's first remix of 'Quoth' isn't much different from the original, aside from its extended length. The other percussive layers – including a new repeated counter-rhythm (perhaps the title's 'wooden thump') – are brought up in the mix, adding a little variety. But really, it's length is inverse to the amount of new ideas it has.

'Bike Pump Meets Bucket' (5:58)
Though the title might make you think it's some experimental *musique concrète* endeavour, the track reveals itself to be a pleasant attempt at downtempo. A swinging drum groove (at least in comparison to the techno rigidity of the rest of the EP) cradles funky Fender Rhodes-esque keys, with the low end boosted to emphasise the hip-hop-inspired production. Aside from the title track, it's the best track on this relatively consistent little EP.

'Quoth (Hidden Mix)' (6:49)

Like the 'Wooden Thump' remix, this version is nearly indistinguishable from the original. Most notably, there is some extra delay on some of the percussion, and the main kick drum pulse is held-off at certain points to increase the building tension for the inevitable drop.

Joyrex J9i & Joyrex J9ii (1993)
Alias: Caustic Window

Personnel:
Richard D. James: Producer, all instruments
Release date: June 1993
Chart placings: Did not chart
Running time: 11:42 (Joyrex J9i); 19:31 (Joyrex J9ii)
Record label: Rephlex Records

James recorded these two new EPs in a limited edition of 300 copies. In a 1993 interview with Simon Reynolds of *Melody Maker*, it's revealed that Warp and Sire (James' US label) 'move too slowly to keep pace with his output': perhaps explaining the brief return to Rephlex here.

The first EP – *Joyrex J9i* – came as a picture disc, with a Roland TB-303 synth on the A-side, and a Roland TR-606 drum machine on the B-side. *Joyrex J9ii* was even more decorated, with the first pressing coming with a t-shirt and Magic Gum candy. The second pressing dropped the t-shirt and replaced the Magic Gum with Fizz Wizz sweets: a typically bizarre James gesture.

Joyrex J9i (1993)
'Humanoid Must Not Escape' (5:41)

The first of these two hardcore acid tracks. Repetitive, unoriginal structure and 303 burbling? Check. Samples that interrupt any flow in the track? Check. Far too long? Also check. There's nothing in this that warrants searching for it – we really have heard it all before.

'Fantasia' (6:01)

This track is on both EPs (it opens *J9ii*), though it's difficult to comprehend why. A maddeningly-annoying 303 mixed with a bludgeoning drum sample and an obnoxious sample that somehow repeats throughout the entire track, does not a good acid-techno track make.

Joyrex J9ii (1993)
'Clayhill Dub' (3:23)

The bass that runs through is suitably dubby, sounding like something Lee 'Scratch' Perry might've done on the 1995 *Super Ape Inna Jungle* LP. But aside from some industrial noise samples that sound like they're lifted from 'Quoth', this track is devoid of substance.

'The Garden of Linmiri' (6:08)
Another slab of hardcore techno, broadly jettisoning the acid instrumentation of the pounding, compressed sound of the *Digeridoo* and *Xylem Tube* EPs. The basic components are as mechanical as ever, with the ambient draping trying its best to cover up the predictable shortcomings. The title refers to the house James lived at in 1986, where most of *SAW 85-92* was made.

'We Are the Music Makers (Hardcore Version)' (3:59)
A more-distorted, much-less-creative reworking of the *SAW 85-92* classic, that bares no musical resemblance to the original. In fact, the only element carried over is the Gene Wilder title sample. The rest is boring and unimaginative techno with a motif that we've heard countless times already.

On (1993)
Alias: Aphex Twin
Personnel:
Richard D. James: Producer, all instruments
Release date: November 1993
Chart placings: UK: 32
Running time: 24:15
Record label: Warp (UK); Sire (US)

James ended 1993 with his most commercially successful project yet. The *On* EP reached 32 in the UK singles chart, which was mainly a by-product of the video made for the title track. Directed by Pulp frontman Jarvis Cocker, the video was ingeniously based on stop-motion animation, involving natural elements, human characters and inanimate objects – to create a chaotic but ultimately warm collage to mirror the track's complexity.

It was heavily rotated on MTV (most prominently on the show *120 Minutes*, which previewed the videos of upcoming artists), which was still in its heyday, meaning that many were exposed to James for the first time. He stated in a 1993 MTV interview that he 'didn't want any computer graphics' in the video. Thankfully, this choice allowed it to remain timeless and unique at the time.

The US version has a different tracklist, with only 'D-Scape' surviving in full. It made up for the time difference by tacking on the 'Reload Mix' of the title track, which also appeared on the *On Remixes* EP, released the same day.

'On' (7:12)
Beginning with plucky synth textures soaked in delay, this piece slowly builds in stature, interweaving countermelodies, soft pads and a fiercely addictive drumbeat. The latter is by-no-means one of James' most complex

or technically advanced. Instead, it serves a greater purpose in its relative simplicity, melding with the rest of the glistening instrumentation rather than taking control of the delicate balance itself.

Flute-like keys flutter into the mix at around the three-minute mark, adding an even-greater sense of wonder, also working with the string sounds to strengthen the ties to James' increasing obsession with modern classical music. It's just fantastic compositional craft all around: a minimalistic triumph.

'73-Yips' (4:19)
Most tracks would struggle to compete with the title track, but the downward turn into this pounding, percussive workout is staggering. It comes off like a more-glitchy and less-solidified remake of 'Quoth' – thus, that track's brute force is lost in the uncomfortable middle ground this track inhabits – between the brutality of something like 'Tamphex', and the technicality of the later 'Buchephalus Bouncing Ball'.

'D-Scape' (6:58)
Focussing mainly on a single melody played on a harp-like synth patch that delves into chromaticism, this is another opportunity for James to demonstrate his classical infatuation. Long, held string notes provide a menacing counterpoint, but the addition of a four-on-the-floor kick drum promises a greater progression that never comes.

'Xepha' (5:46)
This track could slot into *Surfing on Sine Waves* pretty well, considering its whale-call synths wrap around precise, multi-layered drum programming. But it suffers from problems similar to 'D-Scape' in that it's an interesting starting point for development that just doesn't arrive.

On Remixes (1993)
Alias: Aphex Twin
Personnel:
Richard D. James: Producer, all instruments
Reload, µ-Zic: Remixers
Release date: November 1993
Chart placings: Did not chart
Running time: 33:16
Record label: Warp (UK); Sire (US)

As mentioned previously, the same day as the original *On* EP was released, a remix EP was also issued, containing reworked versions of the title track (and, in a quintessential piece of RDJ humour, a remix of 'D-Scape', still titled as 'On') by fellow IDM partners-in-crime Reload and µ-Zic. James contributes two mixes, bringing the total to four.

'On (D-Scape Mix)' (10:42)

Contrary to half of the title, this is a James remix of 'D-Scape'. It's a mixture of shuffling drums and mallet percussion loops, with gently-foreboding synth pads underneath. The drum samples become stale quickly, but the percussion has moments of genuine hypnotic power. The issue is the track's length, which is not justified.

'On (Reload Mix)' (7:06)

On the first actual 'On' remix, guest Reload gives us a house-inspired take. The main riff is filtered and automated, and a slippery deep-house bass line adds more syncopation, highlighted by the machine-gun drums. This drifts into a more subdued section, before coalescing back into the main theme. It's a very pleasant version of a great track.

'On (µ-Zic Mix)' (8:43)

My personal favourite 'On' remix, µ-Zic's reworking strips it to its basic elements in order to infuse more fantastically-crystalline countermelodies. The entire thing inclines towards a minor tonality, mainly thanks to those yearning synth motifs that any synth pop band would die for.

The warping bass gives a greater sense of momentum, while the drums are as punchy as ever. It's just as accomplished as the original, if not better.

'On (28 Mix)' (6:53)

The final remix is by James, and foreshadows the desolate ambience of *SAW Volume II*, bearing no resemblance to the original. *Twin Peaks*-esque electric pianos swirl amongst the lonely keyboard chimes, which – in their lingering drones – amalgamate to create a prototype canvas of the triple album that was to follow.

Bradley's Robot (1993)
Alias: Bradley Strider

Personnel:
Brad Strider: Producer, performer
Release date: 1993 (Month unknown)
Chart placings: Did not chart
Running time: 25:18
Record label: Rephlex Records
All music by Brad Strider (Richard D. James)

The first release under the Bradley Strider alias – ostensibly an outlet for James' more-straightforward techno creations – was a typically mysterious project. The original bore no track titles or credits. (Three were later titled when included in the 2015 Soundcloud Dump). But it did contain a large poster that displayed a silver Rephlex logo on a green background. You win some, you lose some, I suppose.

'NgaiModu' (5:54)

A synth imitating a gamelan-like instrument begins this EP, giving way to muffled, clipped kick drums and bike-chain cymbals. The forgettable rhythm section notwithstanding, the tribal instrumentation – augmented to include droning woodwinds – is a unique texture that brings forth a welcome contrast to James' usual sound palette.

'Leaving Home' (7:40)

More in the vein of a Polygon Window track than 'NgaiModu', 'Leaving Home' takes its time to unravel a string of syncopated piano chords, delayed and detuned electric piano, and the phased murmurs of a kick drum and shakers. It gets the job done as a minimal techno track, though it doesn't allow itself any further exploration to counter its anonymity.

'Linmiri' (5:54)

'Linmiri' – while being geographically linked – is a lot less abrasive than its Caustic Window companion. As a matter of fact, by using a shuffling beat coupled with a bell-like bass line, it runs with the quieter tendencies 'Leaving Home' began to show off. Bolstered by haunting ambient pads and twinkly keys, the composition overall is more nuanced than anything else on this project.

'Untitled' (5:50)

Hard-edged techno drums in the ascendancy of the *Quoth* EP grace this closer but are quickly hindered by the muted, overly-wet production. Crawling through tropes from his other atonal, percussion-focussed tracks, it's the sort of thing James could do in his sleep: and that's not a compliment.

Album: Selected Ambient Works, Volume II (1994)
Alias: Aphex Twin

Personnel:
Richard D. James: Producer, synthesizer, writer
Release date: March 1994
Chart placings: UK: 11
Running time: 156:37 (CD); 166:38 (Vinyl); 177:57 (Website)
Record label: Warp (UK); Sire (US)

It's apt that the most mysterious and lysergic Aphex Twin release was founded in lucid dreaming. It's well known that James survived on a maximum of two hours of sleep per day to minimise his time not working and to get to the stage where – as he put it in a 1993 interview with Simon Reynolds of *Melody Maker* – 'your mind starts getting scatty like you're senile. You do unpredictable things, like making tea but pouring it in a cereal bowl'. As a result of this hypnagogic state, James began lucid dreaming – where you're actually conscious that you're dreaming. He used this ability to write songs in these dreams, and then wake up and play them in real life.

This technique, combined with his synaesthesia – in which one can interpret music as colours and images – creates the album's hazy and deeply-mystifying landscapes. Each is represented by a picture in the vinyl gatefold, most of which are obscured or blurred, representing James' neurological connections with image and sound, and the woozy, dream-like feeling such associations conjure. The fact that all but two tracks have a title (originally just 'Blue Calx', but the 2019 *Peel Session 2* EP confirmed track two was called 'Radiator'), further embeds the concept of dream states and the way we forget many things that we dream about.

Another important feature of the album artwork is the littering of several pie charts across the back cover and record labels. Over the years, fans have drawn links between these and the images displayed inside, reasoning that the sizes of the pie-chart pieces correspond to the track lengths. Therefore, the images represent the titles based on the charts in the corner of each. I will be using these fan-made titles (which now are mostly accepted as fact) for our convenience.

Despite the sheer effort put into this mammoth album, at the time, it was seen as a riposte to James' signing to US label Sire, and was a deliberately uncommercial follow-up to his prior acclaimed works. Much of the press also thought so. Seen through the prism of today's near-unanimous praise for the LP, the critical division it caused upon release is staggering. In the *Village Voice* in 1994, Robert Christgau slated the album: 'These experiments are considerably thinner ... and more static ... than the overpriced juvenilia on the import-only Volume 1'. Conversely, Simon Reynolds was effusive in his *Spin* review: 'You're rarely conscious that James is using analogue synths, samplers and sequencers. More often, it's like he's playing acoustic instruments from the distant future or an alien civilisation'.

These two examples alone demonstrate the album's polarising nature, and that its turn toward soundscapes and mood pieces can be seen as technically accomplished and emotionally resonant, as well as lazy and boring. You could say these multiple interpretations of the music hark back to the many differing and often opposing meanings drawn from the dreams that drove the album into existence. It's perhaps one of the few albums to reach Brian Eno's original intention of ambient music: to be 'as ignorable as interesting' (from the liner notes of his seminal 1975 work *Ambient 1: Music For Airports*, which clearly had a large influence on James). This quality ensures that its power to simultaneously shock, connect and haunt, has stood – and hopefully will continue to stand – the test of time. Being a project completely disassociated from any era, its approach to memory and its dream fragmentation can apply to any life or experience, whether it's the darkest crevices, the most idyllic landscapes, or – most likely – both at once.

'Cliffs' (7:27)

A simple three-note melody introduces the album, intercepted by heavily delayed vocal samples. The major tonality of the repeated phrase, coupled with the childlike samples, gives the piece a sense of innocence – only the slow melting of the notes as they decay – causing them to distort peripherally suggests any menace. A plucky melody joins in, also treated with delay, allowing the components to float without a true sense of tempo – adrift in a dream state, if you will. The track climaxes softly – the pads removed to leave the plucked synth notes to naturally weave around each other's decaying tails until they descend into muffled silence. It's a phenomenal starting point for the album, and is one of the album's few lighter moments overall.

'Radiator' (6:34)

One of only two tracks given titles on the original album, the resonant, percussive timbres of the keys that arrive at around 1:30 suggests the sound of a radiator. It mostly veers into microtonality – i.e. reaching the notes that lie between normal notes and surprisingly, there's the hint of a distant beat at some points. This reinforces the idea of noise and melody in non-musical objects, posing the idea that the 'ambient' of the album title links more to the ambience of daily life.

'Rhubarb' (7:44)

This is the album's most well-known piece, mainly due to the yearning, spectral melody that peacefully lingers over the entire track. It's difficult to distinguish what instruments James is imitating – despite the fleeting presence of woodwind and strings, when combined, only impressionistic sound remains. The gradual fading-in-and-out of the higher countermelody alongside the tear-jerking intervals formed by the meeting of both phrases, is redolent of Eno's similarly emotionally-potent 'Discreet Music'. However, 'Rhubarb' is resolutely unique in its ability to implant its stylings in a fog removed from the present, past, or even the future, to form an emotional connection with the listener.

'Hankie' (4:39) (Not included on the CD issue)
A return to the haunting atmospherics of 'Radiator', delving even deeper into a general sense of foreboding. Unsettling sounds echo around the stereo spectrum, while a lonely church organ, floats in the background. By the end, the mix is consumed by bass oscillations produced through the meeting of all the constituent parts' deep tones.

'Grass' (8:55)
By this point, melody is strung over the compositions like torn drapes hanging at the back of the mix. The flanged creaks of a solitary drum are more like sound effects than any kind of pulse, settling in the left ear to ominously pound as the twilight-like noises bleed together. Though the title seems to link with the idyllic 'Cliffs', the musical elements all suggest a place of deep-rooted emptiness and loneliness; the copious drum reverb revealing the dearth of life. The fact that the track is content to ebb and flow gives the impression that this work has been playing for a long time before we start listening in.

'Mould' (3:31)
Creepy voice samples echo throughout most of this piece – distorted and rendered as the closest thing to a main melodic instrument the track possesses. Some disjointed organ-like pads resonate alongside this, whilst a low bass anchors the track to a consistent rhythm. The title's natural imagery acts as a microcosm for the way the piece groups the tones of 'Cliffs' and 'Grass' together, using vocals in a much more unsettled context.

'Curtains' (8:51)
A sinister chromatic melody repeats continually; the keys being of a music-box quality, reinforcing the corruption of seemingly innocent motivic ideas. Frail synth washes support this part of the piece, but the main draw is the upper-register piano that accents the murk drowning the sounds in haunting atmospherics. Aside from the stalwart, underlying melodic element, the rest of the piece seems deliberately vaporous: highlighting the contrasts inherent in the sound world crafted here.

'Blur' (5:08)
The first in the 'Blur' trilogy of pieces scattered through the LP, surprises immediately by possessing a strong, up-front beat which chordal electric

piano in the left ear follows closely. Woodwind-like pads fade in, and submerged grand piano later colours the mix. The attention-grabbing pulse hides the fact that though the track is still good, it's one of the more inconsequential ones here.

'Weathered Stone' (6:54)

Yet another rigid beat provides the focal point, making this piece the greatest reminder of the sound of *SAW 85-92*. In fact, the phone-dialling timbre of the lead, paired with the bubbling intonation of the sub-bass, could easily fit on that album – it sounds eerily like 'Ageispolis' in its instrumental palette. Despite this, the album production is firmly consistent – particularly the chamber reverb and its juxtaposition to the dry drum loop and left-channel melody.

'Tree' (9:58)

This is one of the album's longest tracks, beginning with a gargantuan drone that enters and decays. The ethereal, sustained piano chimes quiver at the foghorn-level magnitude of its bass presence. By the halfway mark, the drone begins to oscillate and change shape, becoming even more viscerally crushing in the low end as keys circle around unsettling note combinations in the high end. In contrast, choir-esque pads ride on top of this alteration, creating new intervals between the terrifying dronal amalgamation. It's certainly a contender for the LP's most discomforting piece.

'Domino' (7:18)

This title is extremely apt, as the piece revolves around a single synth line immersed in delay. Each repetition sets off a domino effect, the following phrase differing depending on the one beforehand. This stops the piece becoming monotonous or drab, since there's little decoration aside from this one musical element (except for a clarinet-type drone interjection about two-thirds of the way through). Despite the track's length, it doesn't fully dilute the potency of that creative melody.

'White Blur 1' (2:43)

Closing the first disc of the CD version is this continuation of the 'Blur' trilogy. It mainly consists of lonesome wind chimes echoing over numerous voice samples – some pitched up and distorted in order to make them seem frighteningly unnatural. It's as spine-chilling as many of the other pieces here, but given its length and construction, is inevitably less fleshed out than those other tracks.

'Blue Calx' (7:20)

Aside from 'Radiator', this is the album's only other track given a title. It was written in 1992 for the compilation *The Philosophy of Sound and Machine*.

According to the Aphex Twin website, it was the last track recorded at James' home studio Linmiri. At that time, it was released under the alias Blue Calx, making it James' only release under that pseudonym. It begins similarly to 'Tha' – using reverb-heavy noise bursts, on top of which soothing pads map out a graceful chord progression.

Unlike many of the other pieces here – where traditionally-happy or pleasant motifs are subverted – 'Blue Calx' takes the omniscient thrum of the metronomic sound effects and places a gentle, calming melody above it, to actually remove some of the menace at the heart of the composition, and provide a moment of subdued respite in the middle of a continuously-bleak record.

'Parallel Stripes' (8:00)

Another example of James' tendency towards drone, 'Parallel Stripes', quickly progresses from a low rumble to a giant slab of sound. The latter results in the listener's brain attempting to find changes in the stable sound, revealing hidden oscillations and intervals and causing different interpretations to immediately be found. The piece wholeheartedly delves into this, providing a steady dronal output, over which octave leaps are layered until the sound's sheer scale overdrives the mix. It links back to the notion of dreams and our differing views on their meanings, expressing this through the purest sound possible.

'Shiny Metal Rods' (5:33)

The starting beat sounds like it's buried underneath layers of sand and grit before being overrun by water. The distortion and phasing effects provide a further reinforcement of the subscription to the noises of nature. These changes are especially important when considering that little else embellishes this foundation. It adds credence to the proposition first mentioned in the 'Radiator' section, that the 'ambient' of the title applies less to that genre's musical applications and more to capturing the surrounding world's vibrations and tonal (or atonal) features.

'Grey Stripe' (4:45)

Wind sounds populate this immediately frightening composition, accompanied by creaking and scratching synth arpeggios, altered until any tonality has been fully extracted. Along with the 'White Blur' duology, it's probably the most avant-garde work here. There is no melodic presence drifting through: not even a drone. Instead, we are treated to a proto-dark-ambient selection of Dalek-ship synth bubbles and freezing cold noise interjections more akin to muffled screaming or train-track screeching than any recognisable instrument. Despite being one of the less-renowned pieces here, it's arguably one that was most influential on future ambient subgenres.

'Z-Twig' (2:05)

The album's shortest track, but by no means does it have the least substance. In fact, the chipper, delayed keyboard scales are a lighter mirror image to the cascades in 'Domino', as fleeting as they may be. Soon, the bass and higher chirps join the call-and-response, culminating in an all-too-brief segment where the components diverge in a delicate melodic formation, fading into the ether like Kraftwerk's similarly-dense 'Franz Schubert'.

'Windowsill' (7:16)

The combination of flute sounds and fast hand percussion gives this piece a tribal feeling. Everything is in a woozy state, due to the tape delay causing each phrase to be drawn out and brought into the realm of microtonality. The main parts change little throughout, save for some miscellaneous flute notes, leaving it as one of the album's less-satisfying curios.

'Stone in Focus' (10:11) (Omitted from CD pressings due to 80-minute limit)

This may just be James' best musical creation. On the surface, such a claim might seem ridiculous – the piece is made up of a three-chord motif repeated throughout with a quiet ticking noise in the background, paired with a similarly economical high-pitched countermelody. But it's not the surface-level that really makes this track his crowning achievement, despite its many qualities – it's really about the invisible emotional ties that lie amongst the music.

It's extremely difficult to describe the evocative force that hits you when you listen to this work. There are so many ways to find meaning in those three chords or even the spaces left between them. You find yourself longing for a time that may not have even existed, or maybe a time that has or will in the future. It embodies the atypical nature of the album's production, and also its approach to crafting each of them by cementing its place in not only the period when it was written but any period at all.

In my view, the only complete form of the album possesses this track. Thankfully, it seems I'm not alone in this opinion – in a DJ set at London's Printworks in 2019, James' mixed-in 'Stone in Focus' right after the intense drill-and-bass pinnacle the set reached, signifying a momentary calm before the noise storm of his performance's end. The audience was enraptured – hugging, cheering and crying, all in response to this one humble three-chord progression emerging from the speakers above them. Truly masterful.

'Hexagon' (5:58)

'Hexagon' continues the streak of fantastic pieces, holding the most groovy beat and an earworm of a keyboard loop that holds its own against the growing overdrive on the drums. Reinforcing the classical elements strung throughout the album, a low woodwind sound floats around, giving way to an even-more-pillowy synth tickling the left ear. As with 'Weathered Stone', this track could slot into *SAW 85-92*: perhaps even more easily. This is the one time we're closer to the cleaner production style of *On*, rather than the cavernous crafted sonics of the rest of the pieces. It's James doing what he does best at such a high quality.

'Lichen' (4:15)

We can immediately infer from the opening utopian woodwind notes that this is the apotheosis of James' Eno obsession. While the tranquil soundscapes are drawn from *Music for Airports* and *Discreet Music*, the short-form structure is a template based on *Music for Films*. And indeed, this piece is very filmic. The beauteous warmth of the flute textures – especially when tethered by the mirrored low-end phrasing – suggests a place of natural beauty. The sequencing embellishes this sense of unfiltered loveliness – coming after the cool 'Hexagon' and before the aircraft-hanger noise of 'Spots' – to provide one last moment of audible respite as the record nears its close.

'Spots' (7:09)

Like 'Grey Stripe', this track is more field-recording than keyboard-ambience. Although, the dark well of desolation plunged into as the track progresses is undoubtably the child of James' skill with effects – every single part is drenched in delay and copious reverb, smearing the individual sounds into an unidentifiable pool. On a note on his website, James' identified one of the voice samples as a police interview tape, giving the proceedings an even eerier feel. Altogether, it paints a picture of a scene being watched over time; events unfolding at a languid pace; a smudged snapshot of everyday life.

'Tassels' (7:30)

At the centre of 'Tassels' is a buzzing oscillator produced by the EMS Synthi A, according to James' notes on his website – a faltering radio signal engulfed in phased effects: a transmission from the depths of James' sound world. Swathed in masked ambient bursts, the signal writhes and shrieks, engulfing everything surrounding it for a moment before the benevolent pads push it back. As a corrupted, windswept mood piece, it works well. One could imagine it as the soundtrack to night-time segments of *Twin Peaks: The Return*, though it is longer than it perhaps should be.

'White Blur 2' (11:27)

The final entry in the 'Blur' trilogy, and the album's longest piece. A bastardised organ like the one on 'Radiator', plays a typical skin-crawling motif, as James modifies its pitch to highlight its horror-movie aesthetic. This stays constant, but its surroundings shift, with the entrances and exits of multiple voice snippets, a lot of which are unfortunately repeated *ad nauseum*, reminding me of the grading sampling on 'Tamphex'. It's a shame this atmospherically-underdeveloped piece was drawn out to almost 12 minutes, as it meant the masterful 'Stone in Focus' couldn't fit on the CD issues.

'Matchsticks' (5:41)

This is the final track on most issues of the LP, and a return to form after the disappointing 'White Blur 2'. Filmic synth chords create an immediate sense of drama and intrigue, using a choir-like tone to really underline the unsettling climatic feel the piece is aiming for. Low in the mix, an atonal pulse flickers, adding to the portent the dissonant chords eke out. It's a fantastic album closer, because it highlights the unresolved, sinister qualities privileged throughout. Ironically, it leaves the LP on a complete note by throwing light on the omnipresent thread of uncertainty running through the record – a classic juxtaposition that summarises the latter's intentions in a single six-minute composition.

Website bonus tracks
'th1 (evnslower)' (11:07)

Tacked onto the end of the album's Aphex Twin website version, this track was originally uploaded as part of the Soundcloud Dump in 2015. Its one of the record's most synth-heavy pieces, the main instrument being a thick string ensemble preset of the sort usually favoured by composer Angelo Badalamenti. In fact, the swirling voids of chords are another *Twin Peaks* recall, not unlike Badalamenti's 'Dark Mood Woods'. It's pleasant enough, and has many of the album's hallmarks, though more soundscaping work would've been needed to cement its place on the album

The EPs, Part 4: 1994

GAK (1994)

Alias: GAK

Personnel:
Richard D. James: Producer, all instruments
Release date: June 1994
Chart placings: Did not chart
Running time: 24:26 (Original); 45:25 (Website)
Record label: Warp Records

A strange little project, the *GAK* EP is the only release under this particular alias, and allegedly comes from demos he sent to Warp in 1990. It's one of his most backwards-leaning projects, sourcing its sound from the early bleep techno of Warp labelmates LFO, rather than the ambient or IDM sound James was mining at this time. In 2017, the Aphex Twin website reissued it digitally with more than twice as many tracks.

'GAK 1' (6:39)

Circling around a maddening, repetitive drum-machine loop adorned by a few wayward bleeps before some clunky house piano joins the mix, this track lacks interest. But the comparative variety of musical features make it the best here.

'GAK 2' (6:17)

Another nondescript, minimal entry. The flanged bass bobs along, slotting in with the primitive drum loops without much interest. But the bland production doesn't help at all, making this EP's dearth of creativity even more apparent.

'GAK 3' (5:26)

Almost a carbon copy of 'GAK 2', possessing the same scratchy synth figure and drum part. Being so similar, this track is as uninventive as its predecessor, yet somehow has even less compositional movement, and – in the static-like drums – even more annoyance.

'GAK 4' (6:04)

In its clipped, polyphonic funk, this track could've found a better home on the 2017 *Cheetah* EP (a more accomplished version of this project). Unlike that EP, this production is amateurish at best, though, at least the bass and melodies are more-loose than those from the pieces before it.

Website bonus tracks

'gak police, er 2' (4:28)

Here's another *GAK* track has a substandard mix, tedious rhythm parts and the complete absence of any forward momentum. At least the title makes sense – the loud bleeps in the second half have all the engaging musical qualities of a police siren.

'gak bass, e, +2' (3:29)

This is three-and-a-half minutes of poorly mixed, bass-subsumed, minimal techno with some synth sparkles and burps that add nothing whatsoever to the piece.

'gak5 e, +3' (1:37)

A short piece that ends up being perhaps the best thing from the *GAK* collection. It has a fine glimpse of melody and a few different production touches. Best of all, it doesn't outstay its welcome.

'gak6 e, +3' (5:25)

More of the same uninteresting minimal techno fare. The sole hint at development comes in some volume modulation around two-thirds of the way through. But that only gives way to a louder and, therefore, more-tiresome variation on what's already been set out.

'gak 7 e, +3' (6:00)

What is there to say now? This follows the same set of strict rules that every other *GAK* track bows to – the same instrumental palette, structure and interminable length, with the crucial enjoyable or engaging factors conspicuously absent.

Analogue Bubblebath 4 (1994)
Alias: AFX

Personnel:
Richard D. James: Producer, all instruments
Release date: July 1994
Chart placings: UK: 87
Running time: 26:16 (CD); 25:55 (Vinyl)
Record label: Rephlex Records

Another year, another entry into the ongoing *Analogue Bubblebath* EP series. But this was to become the series' final widespread release. The fifth instalment in 1995 was only pressed in small batches. Released through Rephlex, this project is more-similar to the Caustic Window EPs, considering all its tracks are untitled. As ever, fans created unofficial names, though they are now accepted as the tracks' real monikers, and revolve around the animal noises thought to be heard in each piece. The CD version differs slightly from the vinyl, adding the bonus track (if you can call it that) 'Knievel'.

'Elephant Song' (6:21)

This is presumably named after the track's incessant screeching sound, which returns to the harsh techno of Polygon Window in the overdriven drum parts. Subtle ambient pads sometimes meet the beat noise, but rarely. We're left with a tiresome flexing of James' techno muscle – the grit is there, and the sample's elephantine exasperation thoroughly stomps over any trance-inducing qualities.

'Gibbon' (5:05)

Continuing the techno sound palette of 'Elephant Song', 'Gibbon' finds itself more in line with the hardcore-acid stylings of *Xylem Tube* and the *Joyrex J9* EPs – mainly down to the rigid kick drum and 303 eruptions. Overall, there's little substance. When such does appear, the countless times we've heard it before, considerably dulls its impact.

'Cuckoo' (6:04)

A stylistic switch-up, 'Cuckoo' is a vibrant piece of chiptune IDM: almost like a *SAW 85-92* track filtered through a bitcrusher. While it doesn't hit the highs of that album, the bass and melodic elements feed through each other amicably, and the highlighted low-bit melody plays well with the chordal pads. But the animal samples feel superfluous here – shoehorned-in to maintain the theme of the past few tracks.

'Sloth' (8:18)

This is the EP's most accomplished track, focussing on the precise, clinical drum programming that behaves like a subdued version of the kick drums we heard on 'Gibbon'. Melodically, it's nakedly beautiful, using a combination of Aphex trademarks to great effect – stabbing chords in the left channel, languid synth notes in the background, and engaging pillows of percussion. Naturally, these constituents weave their way into different configurations until new patterns of melody and rhythm are revealed: a tactic James has mastered.

'Knievel' (0:28)

This is just a sample from an interview with stunt performer Evel Knievel through a phaser effect.

Album: Classics (1995)
Alias: The Aphex Twin
Personnel:

Richard D. James: Producer, instruments; remixer on both versions of 'We Have Arrived'

Mescalinum United: performer on both versions of 'We Have Arrived'

Release date: January 1995

Chart placings: UK: 24

Running time: 74:04

Record label: R&S Records

Not an album *per se*, but a compilation of most tracks from the *Analogue Bubblebath*, *Digeridoo* and *Xylem Tube* EPs, along with a handful of miscellaneous live performances and remixes. James had nothing to do with the compilation. In fact, he was against it, stating in a 1995 VRPO Radio interview: 'Basically, it's just R&S milking as much money as they can do out of me, 'cause they know I'm not going to give them any more records'. In spite of the concerns, the compilation achieved its goal of introducing more people to James' early music, being a cheaper alternative to searching for the separate singles. This likely contributed to its rise to 24 in the UK album chart. However, 'Isoprophlex' and 'Analogue Bubblebath' were extended, and the titles changed to 'Isopropanol' and 'Analogue Bubblebath 1'. The addition of extra tracks not featured on the other EPs made the compilation a collector's item: compounded by its original issue being pressed on blue vinyl.

As we've covered most of the tracks here, I'll only discuss those bonus tracks.

'Metapharstic' (4:33)
This originally appeared on the 1992 compilation *Mayday – A New Sound in Techno and House*. It's typical of James' early hardcore acid style, favouring an oppressive atmosphere through copious reverb and booming kick drum. The gargantuan sound prevents it from slipping too much into formulaic patterns, though a similar instrumentation can be found in numerous 1990s Aphex tracks.

'We Have Arrived (Aphex Twin QQT Mix)' (Mescalium United, Aphex Twin) (4:23)
The first of two remixes here of the pioneering Mescalinum United piece. It's regarded as the first hardcore techno track, so it makes sense that James would be interested in reworking it. Sadly, this remix is a jumbled mess of industrial drums and sound effects, alternately diving into techno rhythms. The not-altogether-comfortable mix of the two, makes for a watered-down version of the original.

This and the 'TTQ Mix' were originally issued on a joint R&S single with producer The Mover. This mix was later included on the *26 Mixes for Cash* remix compilation in 2003.

'We Have Arrived (Aphex Twin TTQ Mix)' (Mescalium United, Aphex Twin) (5:07)

A much groovier variant of the previous remix, switching out the stuttering shreds of kick drum for a more-consistent breakbeat. The industrial elements also play a lot better in this more fluid context, becoming an integral part of the musical tapestry rather than being draped over it as they were in the 'QQT Mix'. It's definitely the best of the two remixes here.

'Digeridoo (Live in Cornwall, 1990)' (6:20)

Essentially what the title suggests: a live version of the track that made James famous. It's faithful to the original, with little indication that it was played in a live setting. Ultimately disposable, it acts as a bookend to the compilation, which began with the studio version. It hasn't lost any of its menacing qualities, either.

Album: ...I Care Because You Do (1995)
Alias: Aphex Twin

Personnel:

Richard D. James: Producer, all instruments

Release date: April 1995

Chart placings: UK: 24

Running time: 63:45 (Original); 107:22 (Website)

Record label: Warp Records

In 1995, James released his third major studio album under the Aphex Twin name. He'd been crafting this project for some time. Each track is given a date corresponding to when it was written. Most were created with analogue equipment in James' studio at 36 Clissold Crescent in Stoke Newington. *...I Care Because You Do* (which from this point on will be shortened to *ICBYD* for convenience) is the last album James made with primarily analogue production methods. Many tracks are also anagrams of 'Aphex Twin' or 'The Aphex Twin', showcasing more of James' playful side, despite the darkness of some of the tracks.

The classical influence that permeated *SAW Volume II,* returns in full force, contrasting heavily with the abrasive ferocity of the percussive programming – a combination of features old and new, recontextualised in a sometimes frightening – and other times beautiful – context. It's no surprise then that renowned modern-classical composer Philip Glass was happy to collaborate with James: re-recording 'Icct Hedral' (which owes a great debt to Glass' work) for the *Donkey Rhubarb* EP. In a 2013 Red Bull Music Academy interview, Glass said, 'What I liked about (James' music) was that I liked it and didn't understand it'.

This EP summarises the unique qualities of James' work at the time, fusing two disparate genres in a way that allowed aspects of both to shine through while maintaining a careful balance. The critical consensus displayed this, being unanimously positive, as opposed to the divisive *SAW Volume II*. *Rolling Stone* likened *ICBYD* to 'classical music for a generation raised on samplers', while *Entertainment Weekly* reckoned it 'creates sounds that are simultaneously comforting and scary': another encapsulation of James' contrast-heavy genius.

Arguably, the album's most memorable aspect is its artwork, and specifically, the cover painted by James himself – a nightmarish self-portrait that does away with the anonymity of previous Aphex projects and begins a trend of James inserting his leering face into his graphic design. It subverts the notion of the electronic auteur remaining hidden from the listener's view. In contrast, James actively forces you to recognise the music's disturbing traits before having heard it – something the original vinyl issue compounded through the inclusion of a poster and bag adorned with the same terrifying image.

'Acrid Avid Jam Shred (1994)' (7:38)

The album starts with a firm beat and a low atonal drone (prefiguring the one that will run throughout 'Ventolin'). It slowly unfolds with extra percussion added every few bars until it becomes a sluggish, swinging downtempo groove. In fact, the entire piece mirrors the gradual revelation of the complete rhythm section, with the entrance of tranquil pads, dub-like snare flams and subtle sub-bass runs culminating in an excellently musical tapestry.

Each and every part fits together to form a foolproof whole, nothing seeming out of place, despite of the tonal clashes. For example, the colouring of electronic whirring and the slurred, theremin-like synth that arrives halfway through may at first seem musically opposed, but in context, they complement each other beautifully. It's an impressive start, encapsulating the balance between delicacy and force that's maintained throughout the album.

'The Waxen Pith (1993)' (4:49)

The first of many songs with anagrams as titles, 'The Waxen Pith' also introduces the classical elements that infuse the LP. An electronic string quartet plays a lovely, ambiguous melody, mainly circling around the violin's dance between close and separated intervals. On top of this, sits acidic, burbling percussion. The low-end bounces, while the spray of the hi-hat, bursts in-and-out randomly, strengthening the ties to James' older forms of improvisation. Sometimes the string melody to lapses into chromaticism – indicating some disquiet stemming from the machines the album is deeply beholden to.

'Wax the Nip (1990)' (4:19)

A compressed, frenetic drum loop torn straight from *Classics,* immediately bludgeons us. But the fractured, resonant melody uncovers a more romantic side to James' compositional skills, despite being juxtaposed by the intense regularity of the drums surrounding it. In this way, it demonstrates that James can use scale in different ways. The giant, reverb-laden string effects alongside the hard-hitting drums indicate the effects of performance in two culturally-divergent scenarios.

'Icct Hedral (Edit) (1994)' (6:07)

One of James' most nakedly terrifying creations, 'Icct Hedral', is true horror movie soundtrack material. First and foremost, the sound modulations of the drum rhythm, drill into the listener's brain with the timbre of nails on a chalkboard: essential in conveying its dark atmosphere. But the true star is the mighty orchestral wall behind it, where we hear the musical DNA of Philip Glass running through – from the disjunct, dissonant intervals to the woodwind embellishments. Altogether, there's an inescapable mood of impending doom that few other tracks in James' catalogue achieve.

'Ventolin (Video Edit) (1994)' (4:29)

This is the album's most infamous song, mainly down to the ear-piercing dentist-drill whine that anchors the entire track. It's apt, considering Ventolin is another name for the asthma drug Salbutamol, which notoriously causes tinnitus. The aural experience puts the listener straight into that scenario – an example of James' willingness to push his audience's musical boundaries. By the end, the wince-inducing beat subsumes the mix even more, consuming the rest of the musical pieces until only the merciless buzzing is audible – as if we've journeyed through the progressive worsening of the condition over a condensed four-minute stretch.

'Come On You Slags! (1990)' (5:44)

Another pretty disturbing track, particularly the uncontrollable oscillations of the lead melody and phased repetition of the title. The incessant placement of that sample adds to the piece's off-kilter and nauseous feel, most prominent in the whirlwind pace of the breakbeat: especially when it bounces across the stereo spectrum. Despite the menace inherent in each segment, it's clear this was one of the album's earliest-written tracks since it eschews much of the classical influence for a complex and vulgar reinterpretation of the early Aphex Twin material.

'Start As You Mean to Go On (1993)' (6:05)

A heavily compressed breakbeat that would sit comfortably on *Xylem Tube,* pulsates relentlessly at the start, as blissful, ambient drops, peal behind. Soon enough, the latter falls away, leaving the drums to throb and clang. This doesn't last long though, with those gorgeous, woozy decorations returning to outline a tentative, disjointed melody in contrast. Though the fusion of the glacial and hyperactive does *go on* for too long, the track presents the heart of the split running through the album, time after time.

'Wet Tip Hen Ax (1994)' (5:17)

This inhabits a strange, slightly nightmarish and uncanny valley, due to the artificial aspect of the use of synths to replicate *real* instruments. But this is precisely what makes it unique. Sprays of percussion and drips of bass can be fed into orchestral layers, to innovative and pleasing effect; dramatic string melodies and woodwind trills can be edited to seem even more bone-chilling while the production ekes out a watery, squelchy texture from all the instruments used. The fact that all of this works as well as it can at the same time, is something to be applauded.

'Mookid (1994)' (3:51)

'Mookid' is one of the most underrated (and one of my all-time favourite) Aphex Twin tracks. Along with 'Alberto Balsalm', it's probably the album's biggest outlier, being focussed on a tear-jerking melody and an indescribable drum rhythm (sound-wise) that's the closest descendant from Kraftwerk's 'Numbers'. The combination of frail, reversed-sounding ambient segments and alien, near-vocal synth qualities in the left channel (not to mention the piano riff that's disarming in its simplicity) is breathtaking. Like the feelings unearthed by 'Stone in Focus', 'Mookid' unravels more of that melancholy to remind you how capable James is of representing washes of emotion in musical form.

'Alberto Balsalm (1994)' (5:10)

This contender for the most famous Aphex track, earns that prestige easily. Constructing a groove on a sample of an ammunition box opening, a plaintive and plucky melody dances around the metallic clangs and scissor-like sound effects, to create an exquisite reinterpretation of *musique concrète*. The melodic elements are – like those in 'Mookid' – perfectly balanced between euphoria and sadness. And the sections where multiple theme variations in the upper and lower synth registers come together are stunningly hypnotic, to say the least.

If nothing else, 'Alberto Balsalm' encapsulates James' growth as an artist to that point, embedding the techniques he'd finetuned for four years, in the perfect meeting of every single one of them. Simultaneously simple, knottily complex, longing and content, it's the distillation of James' exploration of opposites into pure *feeling* and music.

'Cow Cud Is a Twin (1994)' (5:33)

A journey into field-recorded sound-play is how I would sum up 'Cow Cud Is a Twin'. It begins with shouts of 'Alright?' and the slamming of doors – the latter emphasised further with the swift fade-out-and-in of the repeated groove, like doors opening and closing. The crafted groove is stellar – dirty, bass-driven funk, punctuated by the vibrant clang of a snare that Sly Stone or Betty Davis would be proud of. James litters this rhythmic triumph with ethereal synths and noise, overdriving some mix points to sound as if buried in a different era entirely. Solemn vocal chants, piano ostinati and James' trademark synth swells, amalgamate into a mesmerising display of rhythmic flow.

'Next Heap With (1993)' (4:43)

The admittedly chintzy organ sound initially promises a humorous close to a pretty humorous album, but the staccato bowing of a string quartet introduces a greater sense of drama and occasion to the proceedings. Brass makes an appearance – giving the piece an almost military importance – though the dissonant chords and intervals stop it from lapsing into cliché. Unlike 'Actium' or 'Matchsticks', 'Next Heap With' doesn't feel much like a finale. It isolates only one part of the album's sound, seemingly promising more by leaving the conclusion purposefully incomplete, as though it's just a taster for even-more-prodigious things to come.

Website bonus tracks (in order of album appearance)
'efil pearls , e, +4' (5:57)
This track can be placed firmly in the *ICBYD* era, thanks to its combination of funky drum patterns, minimalist piano ostinati, and dark sub-bass rattling the bottom of the mix. It's certainly weaker than the tracks that made it onto the album – the piano parts are far less memorable or intricate, and the flanged sounds become tiring after a while.

'winding road , e, +4.1' (3:15)
This bonus revolves around the layering of surprisingly pop-orientated chromatic progressions, within a clave-like rhythm. Small hints of the album's classical side seep in with piano and bowed-bass interjections. The track is an engaging curio, but its short length means there isn't much room for sustaining the attractive balance it has between its arpeggiators and synths.

'with my family (48k) *' (4:11)
One of the few continuously gorgeous tracks to emerge from the *ICBYD* sessions, this threads the cycling, stacked arpeggios of 'winding road' to much improved melodic and trance-inducing effect. As the homely and cosy title suggests, the track has an innocence that's absent for most of the album. Its clipped and enchanting naivety results in it feeling out of place on the main LP. Despite this, I'm glad this plaintive gem hasn't been lost in James' mental archives.

'consta-lume' (7:04)
Slowly constructing itself, 'consta-lume' is a strange, lopsided creation. Though its structure may have some similarity to 'Acrid Avid Jam Shred', the groove is stiff, and the track prioritises ambience over rhythm. Large disembodied pads that would seem more at home on *SAW Volume II*, hang over the spongy drums, gracefully filling out the space before the whir of a mechanical synth ushers the track out. Nevertheless, a dark atmosphere peripherally suffuses it throughout. Sporadically alluring, the track tends to drag at points, possessing only some overtly unique parts.

'merry maidens e, ru, ec, +4' (2:18)
A short, chiptune-style track that reintroduces purely melodic aspects from 'winding road' and 'with my family'. Like the latter, it's a modest piece, lasting only two minutes, and wasting no time introducing and developing its glitchy lead melody. The bass clashes with the blissful melodic components, adding a layer of James' usual musical juxtapositions.

'no cares (48k) *' (2:49)
Another short, peaceful piece in the bonus tracks' beauteous lineage. Woozy synth pads ride gently over a relaxed beat, as reversed keys contribute further

to the laid-back feel. Sparkling, miniature arpeggios ascend and descend beautifully alongside all of this. The sole disturbance comes with a one-bar drum break emphasising the title's claim to having no worries at all.

'consciousness utopia' (7:18)

A familiar squelchy beat indicates we might be returning to the album's percussive-central sound, but the bittersweet woodwind bursts put a stop to that. It actually turns out to be another superbly melancholy track, with stacks of woodwind brought to the fore in the form of soothing pads and poignant melodic phrasing. As usual, sound modulation plays a large part in the repetitive rhythm section's sustained interest, so as to retain the transfixing feel the circling composition grasps from the beginning.

'sekonda e, +2' (10:44)

If 'Icct Hedral' was James' Philip Glass tribute, 'sekonda' is his homage to one of the other epochal modern-classical innovators: Steve Reich. Right from the start, cycles of melody and rhythm begin to take shape – whether that's the block piano chords, the beat's scratchy delay or the string and woodwind arpeggios. Like many of Reich's most beguiling, mesmerising works, 'sekonda' builds a mountainous presence from little – demonstrated in the payoff of the randomness of each cycle beginning to naturally form into something more structured by the piece's close.

The EPs, Part 5: 1995
Ventolin (1995)
Alias: Aphex Twin
Personnel:
Richard D. James: Producer, all instruments
Mum: Vocals
Release date: March 1995
Chart placings: UK: 49
Running time: 26:21 (Original); 30:37 (Website)
Record label: Warp Records (UK only); Sire/Elektra

As befits James' sense of humour, the single from *ICBYD* wasn't 'Alberto Balsalm' or 'Mookid', but the notoriously abrasive 'Ventolin'. Two EPs (issued as a double in the US) were spun off from this track, gathering a further 11 different versions of it (the album mix included as the first track on both). Similar to the *On Remixes* EP, a large percentage of the reworkings on both this and the *Ventolin Remixes* EP bore little resemblance to the original versions. Most are named after places in Cornwall. The rest link to the theme of asthma and the drugs used to control it.

Perhaps surprisingly, the EP reached the UK top 50, though that was probably a by-product of the single's video rather than people's sudden acclimatisation to the track itself. The video – directed by Steven Doughton and Gavin Wilson – shows a woman trapped inside an elevator while an inhaler with the Aphex Twin logo emerges and disappears inside a packet, reminding us of the track's purpose to simulate the side effects of the asthma drug Salbutamol.

'Ventolin (Salbutamol Mix)' (5:46)
This is an extended mix of the *ICBYD* version. It retains the overpowering force of the original but tends to get too repetitive and monotonous by the time it gets past the original length. This longer form dilutes the shock value a little.

'Ventolin (Praze-An-Beeble Mix)' (3:21)
The original's oppressive nature is here switched out for a piece of glitchy post-industrial IDM. It's completely percussion focussed, except for a treated vocal sample of James' mother Lorna, laughing. The latter part is a clever, somewhat heartwarming production choice. The other parts of the piece seem unremarkable in comparison.

'Ventolin (Marazanvose Mix)' (2:10)
A hip-hop-inspired cut and a display of James' proficiency for forming a consistent groove. This aspect is especially worthwhile, considering the production style places it in line with the psychedelic and abstract beats of Madlib or J Dilla. So, it's unfortunate that the second half of this two-minute

fragment is made up of obnoxious samples that indicate a lack of ideas for how to develop the beat.

'Ventolin (Plain-An-Gwarry Mix)' (4:37)

Seemingly a nascent 'Cow Cud Is a Twin', with hints of the sub-bass power and swinging hypnotism of the final version. It's transparently underdeveloped, with different samples to the album cut, and a contrasting, more-playful tone than the album version's ethereal drift. Overall, it's fun to see the gestation process for one of James' tracks, but it definitely doesn't replace the final version in the slightest.

'Ventolin (The Coppice Mix)' (4:35)

An almost microtonal lead melody climbs in amongst the knotty drum programming. The machine-gun kick drums are a premonition of the organised rhythmic chaos found all over the *Richard D. James Album*. Decayed synths become more and more glitched and crazed, exposing the intentionally shaky hook. Having said that, the track doesn't get too sonically intense, remaining laid-back for the most part.

'Ventolin (Crowsmengegus Mix)' (5:52)

Sparkling delayed synths replace the original's horrifying atmosphere with a more-charming sound palette, despite the return of the heavily compressed drums from the original mix. At around 1:45, the track changes to a swing beat, and the plucked keys play a rollicking, ascending melody. It's without a doubt the most fun of all these reworks; surprisingly close to glam rock in the steady drums and syncopated melodic aspects.

Website bonus tracks
'hilow (ru, ec, +3)' (2:55)

Continuing the hip hop rhythm from the 'Ventolin (Marazanvose Mix)', this track is deceptively amateurish, at least when considering the muted, faded production. The melodies are gorgeous, their innocent qualities deepened by the worn sound design, making this a buried treasure that deserves more attention.

'ventolin1 un e, ru, ec+2' (1:21)

This is effectively a demo of 'Ventolin', or a prospective alternate mix of it for one of the EPs. It would make more sense as the former, considering it contains the outline of the tinnitus ringing and the embryonic form of the punishing beat. And yet, it seems blatantly unformed.

Ventolin (Remixes) (1995)
Alias: Aphex Twin
Personnel:

Richard D. James: Producer, all instruments
Cylob, Luke Vibert: Remixers
Release date: March 1995
Chart placings: Did not chart
Running time: 26:48
Record label: Warp (UK only); Sire/Elektra

Released simultaneously with the *Ventolin* EP, this remix project mirrored the *On* EP diptych of 1993. Like that release, *Ventolin (Remixes)* contained a handful of very different reworkings of the title track by James himself, and a few selected mixes by musical friends Cylob and Luke Vibert, the latter who has remained a consistent collaborator. In the US, the two *Ventolin* EPs were packaged as a single CD. In the UK, they were released separately, with additional 12"-vinyl options.

'Ventolin (Wheeze Mix)' (7:00)

A corrupted take of the original 'Ventolin' opening, fades into view with massive bass hits resonating behind it. Contrary to the source material, this mix uses the album version's torn-up loop as a rhythmic base to layer new melodies over. Tuneful sounds play motifs, not unlike the creepy lines strung through *SAW Volume II*. But the sonic terror is diluted by the length.

'Ventolin (Carmarrack Mix)' (2:46)

Almost entirely rhythm focused, the 'Carmarrack Mix' has the lo-fi hip-hop DNA of tracks like 'hilow' and 'Ventolin (Marazanvose Mix)'. A groggy, oscillating melody is played on tape-delayed keyboards, sounding like Aphex protégées Boards of Canada, but – annoyingly – without the quiet uncanniness and buried terror that duo can extract from similar equipment.

'Ventolin (Probus Mix)' (4:10)

The 'Probus Mix' utilises a near-identical instrument array as the preceding remix, but to more impactful effect. The tonal aspects shine through greater than on that track, multiple melodic ideas being played simultaneously, sometimes in the pentatonic area, James sometimes favours. The backing has a stop/start quality that's not as funky as the hip-hop beats of other 'Ventolin' interpretations, but the numerous switches suit this mix's structurally-defined nature.

'Ventolin (Cylob Mix)' (James, Cylob) (5:01)

Cylob's take – the first 'Ventolin' remix – stays partially in a vaguely industrial setting, but the rest is taken back to IDM. The bleeping, slurred synths are thrown together with the technicality of the drum skitters, and rounded synth pads accent the syncopated spaces between beats, placing the basic track in a more overtly-dramatic setting.

'Ventolin (Deep Gong Mix)' (James, Luke Vibert) (6:17)
In Vibert's remix, we return to the percussive backbone of *ICBYD*, fitting a hip-hop groove underneath the tuned-mallet segments. It's one of the more-commercial conversions here – the beat able to slot in with the downtempo movement: for example. Nevertheless, some elements – such as the crowd samples – seem incongruous and not entirely necessary.

'Ventolin (Asthma Beats Mix)' (1:34)
The final remix is a short one. Like the majority of the adaptations, it has a strong rhythmic foundation, though it's the least creative. A shred of a jazz chord progression (though microtonal) is shown before the track is swept away. It's the most insubstantial remix and my least-favourite – thankfully left to the end to be disposed of.

Donkey Rhubarb (1995)
Alias: Aphex Twin
Personnel:
Richard D. James: Synths, drum programming
Philip Glass: Orchestration (3)
Anne Pope: Recording/mix engineer (3)
Rich Costey: Additional engineer (3)
Producers: Richard D. James (1, 2, 4); Kurt Muncasci and Michael Reisman (3)
Release date: August 1995
Chart placings: UK: 78
Running time: 24:35 (Original); 32:28 (Website)
Record label: Warp Records

As a postscript to the *ICBYD* era, *Donkey Rhubarb* has three new tracks, and an orchestrated reworking of 'Icct Hedral' courtesy of Philip Glass. The two musicians were eager to work together, despite James' lack of formal musical training. In a conversation with Red Bull Music Academy, Glass recalled himelf and James sharing tracks with each other, working on improving and tweaking each other's elements. So, it's not surprising that the *ICBYD* track that draws the most inspiration from Glass' compositional style, is the one they collaborated on.

The title track is notable for having the next music video – introducing another section of James' visual iconography: the Aphex Twin bears. Straddling the delicate balance between adorable and disturbing, the bears play into the amalgamation of cute and slightly deranged that encapsulates the Aphex Twin persona. They were an enduring presence – live shows throughout 1996 typically featured the crowd-pleasing appearance of the bears replicating their suggestive dancing from the 'Donkey Rhubarb' video.

'Donkey Rhubarb' (6:08)

The sickly-sweet steel-drum-powered melody sits alongside the solid force of the uncomfortably loud percussion. Everything feels manic, and the different melodies all seem *too* happy, but maintain the frenzied drive. But there's still time for isolated moments – first, the overlapping harmonies, and closer to the end, the house and techno-inspired percussive breakdown. The latter breaks up the maniacal riff, though its naïve runs seem to be nauseating on purpose to further reinforce the simultaneous apprehension we're meant to feel towards it.

'Vaz Deferenz' (5:50)

The bubbly drum sounds from the title track make a reappearance here, but the rest of 'Vaz Deferenz' forgoes any of that track's (however-oppressive) childlike atmosphere. It has the most in common with the maximalist techno of *Classics* – meaning (annoyingly enough) that it becomes intolerable relatively quickly, leaving any classical-infused darkness behind for a mesh of irksome loops and disorienting percussion.

'Icct Hedral (Philip Glass Orchestration)' (8:06)

Somehow managing to improve on the original's greatness, this version of 'Icct Hedral' marks the height of James' modern-classical obsession. Replacing the nightmarish drums and submerged atmospherics of the original with dissonant choral elements and potent woodwinds and strings, Glass' deft arrangement only brings the original's terrifying sounds into sharper focus. The interjecting, buried electronic bass hits only accentuate the constant, ceaseless menace that suffuses every aspect of the piece.

'Pancake Lizard' (4:31)

An anomaly in James' catalogue, 'Pancake Lizard' is a superb fusion of classical and *real-world* instrumentation with the languid drum groove of the downtempo movement that was becoming popular at the time. It contains acoustic guitar – rare in James' music – its grit adds a rustic, aged feeling, helped by the stalwart strings and worn percussion. The unsettled, questioning melody is surprisingly catchy. At some points, the motifs are almost mere impressions, and the fact that we can latch onto these is a testament to James' confident handle on sound design and melodic craft.

Website bonus tracks
'icct hedral (philip glass dry version+bonus DAT glitches)' (7:55)

The lengthy title is extremely precise – this bonus track is a variant of the 'Icct Hedral (Philip Glass Orchestration)', minus further production touches. The mix is 'dry' since there is no reverb or ambience added to the instrumental layers. Also, the promised 'DAT glitches' are all present, corrupting the song at certain points. Both advertised drawbacks make this a one-listen curio at most.

Bradley's Beat (1995)
Alias: Bradley Strider
Personnel:
Brad Strider: Producer, performer
Release date: September 1995
Chart placings: Did not chart
Running time: 10:53 (First pressing); 12:02 (Second pressing); 6:07 (Third pressing)
Record label: Rephlex Records
All music by Brad Strider (Richard D. James)

The second EP under the Bradley Strider name has proven to be confusing to fans for a number of reasons. Firstly, the EP is said to have been released in 1991, and has the Rephlex catalogue number 001 – indicating it was the label's first release. In fact, the EP was sold in September 1995, and there was no other written indication of the former, and the latter release date was confirmed in a press release. Secondly, the project garnered three separate pressings. The first two included different versions of the B-side, and the third had no groove on the B-side at all.

'Bradley's Beat (Part One)' (6:10)
The sketches out a jumpy techno foundation that James layers with various droopy, sustained synth phrases. Overall, it's mediocre and doesn't offer much to warrant the listener's investment.

'Bradley's Beat (Part Two)' (Version 1) (4:43)
Starting off like a bootleg version of 'Quoth' (vistas of cycling tremolo beats and all), the first 'Part Two' descends back into 'Part One''s mediocrity, as the cliché hi-hat sprays resume control. The vaguely-dissonant chordal motif trading octaves throughout is another hackneyed component that ultimately dissuades you from wanting to listen again.

'Bradley's Beat (Part Two)' (Version 2) (5:53)
This applies a generous dose of distortion to the unfortunately-identical techno beat and whispery, wavering synth melody traipsing around the drums. At its core, the base elements are still as overused and uninteresting as they are everywhere else here, but the slight change in production style at least attempts to correct this.

Hangable Auto Bulb (1995)
Alias: AFX
Personnel:
Richard D. James: Producer, performer

Release date: October 1995
Chart placings: Did not chart
Running time: 24:59
Record label: Warp Records

This is the first of two EPs forming one of James' most influential releases. It's a milestone in his career and in the grander scheme of electronic music, provided the basis for the genre later to be coined drill-'n'-bass. This – and its successor – outline the foundations of the genre's typical features – maddening, fast breakbeats, usually digitally edited to create a skittering or time-stretched effect; simple melodies alongside these complex beats, and multiple musical switches, adding to the sense of complete disorientation and confusion brought on by the whirlwind pace.

Though the nominal name drill-'n'-bass indicates a sidestep from the drum-and-bass compositions gaining severe popularity parallel to James' explorations, it's simultaneously more-unashamedly-technical and dark, while also containing greater vestiges of melody than the genre it was originally birthed from. There's not much demarcation between the sweet, bouncy tune of 'Donkey Rhubarb' being immersed in oppressive drum sounds, and the deceptively-innocent synth phrases of a track like 'Laughable Butane Bob', found in the midst of a percussive battering. Thus, *Hangable Auto Bulb* as a complete project is a nexus point between the analogue contrasts of prior solo works and the mightily-impressive and daunting musical lattices of *Richard D. James Album, Come to Daddy* and beyond.

'Children Talking' (5:16)
Only the idiosyncratic sampling remains from James' earlier projects. This time it's a sample from the BBC series of the same title. When anything originally innocent enters the Aphex world, it's sonically corrupted. Besides the chopped-up drums that rain bullets through the mix, the sample is stretched, sped up, slowed down and phased until it becomes as rhythmic as the percussion itself. Later, a sinister, plucky bass motif glitches into the track, hurtling the listener further into the inescapable darkness that every element resonates.

'Hangable Auto Bulb' (6:46)
The lengthy title track is James' chance to showcase his titanic gift for programming percussion. The rifling of the initially-disparate beats comes together in an airtight semi-swing until it dives into cavernous kick-drum-infested waters just before the halfway mark. James' craft permits the intensely digitised and commanded percussion to have a seeming mind of its own, taking various compositional twists and turns to keep the listener constantly on their toes.

'Laughable Butane Bob' (2:59)

Stationed right next to the most percussion-heavy track is the EP's most melodic piece, with a fantastic descending bass sequence complementing the full synth textures nestled above it and between the demented assault of the snare rolls on either side. It's a pure blend of the best aspects of both contesting sides of the EP series, cramming meticulous changes and returns into barely three minutes.

'Bit' (0:07)

This is a short burst of seemingly time-stretched noise, perhaps meant to act as a transitionary bridge between the opening three tracks and the rest of the EP.

'Custodian Discount' (4:23)

A cheap, vaporous keyboard sound knocks out a trademark subverted James riff, initially pleasant enough, until it hits the sharp final note. The *déjà vu* is somewhat displaced by the addition of a harmony part and shrill synth spikes, and the drums are permitted to carry the middle section into a bass-driven reversed zone as a precursor to the triumphant reintroduction of the two parallel motifs: tying the journey up in a bow.

'Wabby Legs' (5:28)

Wabby is a British slang term for flying insects, like wasps. Perhaps its use here is a self-aware jab at the buzzing drill-'n'-bass beats populating the two EPs. Once again, a cheap preset (this one sounding close to a Stylophone: an early electronic instrument) maps out a simple melody, embellished with clever production tricks implemented when you least expect them. It has a near-identical structure to 'Custodian Discount', with some added pizzazz in the drum department from a tonal percussion breakdown three-quarters of the way through.

Hangable Auto Bulb EP.2 (1995)
Alias: AFX

Personnel:
Richard D. James: Producer, performer
Release date: December 1995
Chart placings: Did not chart
Running time: 9:04
Record label: Warp Records

The concluding part of the *Hangable Auto Bulb* series consists of two remaining tracks. It was released a few months after the original EP. In 2005, Warp compiled the two EPs in a release also titled *Hangable Auto Bulb*, with new artwork that combined the original issues' two coloured labels.

'Every Day' (3:50)

This is another superbly melodic and harmonic track in the vein of 'Laughable Butane Bob', reprising the full, glistening synth textures of that song with a playful yet melancholic motif. The sampling integrates just as well as that of 'Children Talking', though it manages to be less annoying, being a shorter length. It helps that the clattering percussion snugly cradles the chords presented through the bubbling oscillator, and that the progression is genuinely affecting, making this perhaps the most sincere track here.

'Arched Maid Via RDJ' (5:25)

Beginning with a funky crushed-note-inflected riff that could've come from a Parliament or Prince record, 'Arched Maid Via RDJ' proceeds to throw a heap of hooks and melodies at the listener. The drums burst and blast through the mix, which is smothered in layers of plaintive, irresistible motifs that are prototypes for the likes of the later 'Girl/Boy Song' in their density and synergy. Amazingly, the track also manages to cram in at least three musical switch-ups – keeping it in line with the rest of both EPs, and ending them on a stellar note.

Album: Expert Knob Twiddlers (1996)
Alias: Mike & Rich

Personnel:
Richard D. James, Mike Paradinas: Producers, performers
Release date: June 1996
Chart placings: Did not chart
Running time: 57:51 (Original); 86:27 (2016 reissue)
Record label: Rephlex Records
All music by Richard D. James and Mike Paradinis

In some ways, this James and Mike Paradinas (the man behind 'µ-Zic Mix') collaboration is a step backwards from the pioneering drill-'n'-bass of the *Hangable Auto Bulb* EPs. In 1997, Paradinis told *Perfect Sound Forever* that 'it was an updated version of easy-listening and funk': two genres James had only flirted with previously. This is more than a little unfair on the project, considering its intention was presumably to feed both artists' musical creativity and heritage, rather than being a colossal statement piece.

Starting in 1994, the pair worked on the album in a flat in London called Johnnie's. Some songs – such as 'Giant Deflating Football' – are tied to events from the year they were written – that one written during the 1994 FIFA World Cup. Ideas for the album were also sourced in chemicals – Paradinas stating in a feature for *Dummy* that they 'were getting drunk and making tracks', and that they 'took a bit of acid ... and we were coming up with some imagery, like 'Beady Eyes', which is mentioned in one of the tracks'.

The cover is a take on the classic MB Games board-game boxes, depicting Paradinas and James in the middle of a game of Downfall. It highlights the project's non-serious, tongue-in-cheek nature, though the attention to detail ensures it's not completely comedic. The reviews then and since have picked up on the same overarching mood, praising some parts of the album for its kitschy qualities, but criticising others as self-indulgent.

The album was reissued with an extra disc of bonus tracks for its 20th anniversary in 2016.

'Mr. Frosty' (6:51)
The funk influence is clear here, with infectious keyboard portamento straight out of a Sly and the Family Stone album. The sound is as enticing as the ice cream of the title, being a sugary swirl of cushiony pads and fat bass tones as the keys dart from one ear to the other. This track lives up to the intriguing premise of mixing old school funk and easy listening, shining through even more than the trademarks we've come to expect from these artists.

'Jelly Fish' (6:30)
A loop sampled from Francoise Hardy's 1964 song 'Catch a Falling Star' plays throughout, continuing the nostalgic bent of 'Mr. Frosty'. More groovy

keys enter, but the focus is much more on the drums this time around, being higher in the mix, and possessing a greater bottom end. On top drifts a spooky, theremin-like synth and the pitter-patter of a marimba. But sometimes, its like a case of too much being thrown in, resulting in everything becoming too clouded to cut through.

'Eggy Toast' (4:07)
The third food-related item begins with a jazz loop repeating an acoustic bass riff with some sidestick rhythms. This quickly gives way to layers of chiptune synths that transition into a hypnotic flow, dominated by the effortless bass embellishments. The piano reminds us constantly of the eminently-repetitive nature of it all. But at some points, it becomes uncomfortable amid the growing instrumentation.

'Reg' (5:57)
'Reg' commences with a buoyant, vintage, 1960s R&B loop. A wordless vocal sample rides alongside a shrill synth preset, while marimba dances on top. More than any of its predecessors, 'Reg' prioritises the human elements – whistling slots into the groove too, before the flanged keys dive in once again. But it's all a bit anonymous in the context of the tracklisting.

'Vodka' (4:12)
'Vodka' is a rerun of the heavily percussive sounds of *ICBYD* and *Donkey Rhubarb*, with much of the other instrumentation being sidelined in favour of more claustrophobic beats. But we're left without the attractive melodies or classical fusions of those two projects. In contrast, there's only a pile of synth burbles in the background, leaving the rest too exposed for its own good.

'Winner Takes All' (5:44)
A swing rhythm and walking bass line usher in this next track, with a decidedly-chipper vibraphone melody and hip-hop-inspired beat. Standard Aphex synth pads act as a subtle dissonant aspect among the bouncy energy, bringing the joyful motif closer to uneasy darkness, though the unrelenting cycles of horn and keyboard riffs make it a bit tiresome to sit through, unfortunately.

'Giant Deflating Football' (6:22)
So named presumably for the airy, breathy sound effect that passes in and out of the track. Surrounding this, is instrumentation absent of traditional percussion, driven by the distant horns and all-consuming bass. The theremin synth slinks its way back in, adding some textural variety to a fine but ultimately motionless piece that bides its time well enough.

'Upright Kangaroo' (3:31)

A quirky number with a slow percussion build, recycling the automated and precise blips from 'Donkey Rhubarb' and such. A syncopated flow is crafted, weaving in vocal samples and spiky keys for another few minutes until the track closes. It's definitely the least-substantial work here.

'The Sound of Beady Eyes' (7:46)

Similar to 'Mr. Frosty', this consists of mountainous layers of keyboard sounds, slathered in effects, forming an infectious and deeply funky pulse. The drums are simple, and more effective in this context than in the more-uncomfortable material. Swirling, melodic synth lines – some even mimicking brass sounds for a 1980s touch – bring some effective countermelodies, reminding us of the album's original intention to fuse genres.

'Bu Bu Bu Ba' (6:51)

A very slow and languid cut closes the album, cycling around the title phrase that becomes annoying after enough repetition. Due to its length and pacing, it's the LP's least-cluttered track. The horn loops and distorted voices that enter a third of the way through are transfixing, and so is the bubbly synth improvisation. It's a shame the track goes on for so long and wastes its captivating mood by outstaying its welcome.

2016 reissue bonus tracks

'Vodka (Mix 2)' (4:22)

This is an alternate mix of 'Vodka' – but with a more prominent, itchy beat – which only grows in instrumental size as it trundles along. As such, it feels like a more-creative sidestep to the album mix; the retained elements making more sense in this context.

'Portamento Gosh' (2:02)

Competing with the funk and easy-listening elsewhere, this ventures into another older genre – stuffed to the brim with portamento (slides) in a Keith Emerson/Rick Wakeman prog style. Ultimately, it's a fun diversion, though inherently lacking in true substance.

'Waltz' (5:24)

This detailed and dense package takes smaller elements and repeats them in new circumstances. For example, what begins as a clearly-defined melody section, soon fades into abstraction as noise and distortion creeps in at the edges, while delay and reverb push the lovely synths out of focus.

'Brivert & Muonds' (6:18)

A low-slung groove in the vein of 'Cow Cud is a Twin' is piloted by bass and muffled drums. It would make a great hip-hop backing. Sans any memorable wordplay, it joins the heap of predominantly-pleasant yet unsurprising bonus tracks.

'Clissold Bathroom' (0:56)

This is a hazy, distant fragment containing a bass motif that could've plausibly been sourced from *SAW Volume II*, but is without the gradual development and overwhelming dark atmosphere of that seminal record.

'Jelly Fish (Mix 2)' (5:21)

Another alternate mix that – like 'Vodka (Mix 2)' – prioritises the percussion over the originally-more-prominent R&B loop. Unlike that other bonus mix, the drums here are far less interesting, and are immediately overtaken by the remaining elements.

'Organ Plodder' (4:15)

Whereas some tracks on *Expert Knob Twiddlers* may *fuse* the rhythm section with constantly shifting melodic textures, 'Organ Plodder' is all about the latter: the organ taking centre stage. There's a bare-bones kick drum and bass beat, allowing the organ to take off on multiple extended improvisations. It's another very capable track that should've been included with the original ten.

Above: Richard D. James, AKA Aphex Twin, around the time of the *Digeridoo* EP.

Below: A young Richard D. James in a rare photo recently unveiled by legendary photographer Pat Pope. (*Pat Pope*)

AnalogBubblebathVol2

Aboriginal Mix

RabbitCity records ✳002

Left: The label of the *Analogue Bubblebath Vol. 2* EP, the first release under the Aphex Twin alias. (*Rabbit City*)

Right: The first full-length Aphex Twin album, *Selected Ambient Works 85-92*, is an electronic landmark to this day. (*Apollo*)

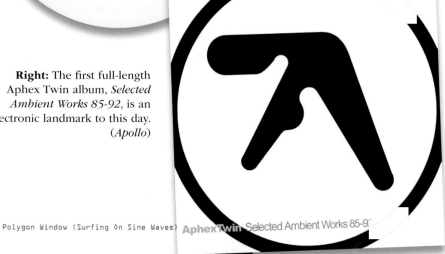

Polygon Window (Surfing On Sine Waves) Aphex Twin Selected Ambient Works 85-9.

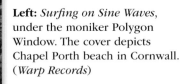

Left: *Surfing on Sine Waves*, under the moniker Polygon Window. The cover depicts Chapel Porth beach in Cornwall. (*Warp Records*)

Right: *Quoth*, the second and final Polygon Window release, had its cover photographed in London's Embankment station. (*Warp Records*)

Left: The *On* EP: James' most successful project so far, thanks to MTV's rotation of the 'On' music video directed by Jarvis Cocker. (*Warp/Sire Records*)

Right: *Selected Ambient Works Volume II*: a two-hour dark ambient voyage, spurred on by James' lucid dreaming and synaesthesia. (*Warp/Sire Records*)

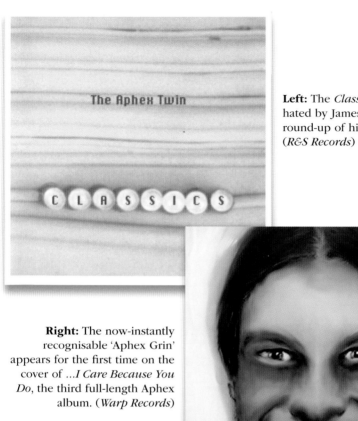

Left: The *Classics* compilation: hated by James, but a handy round-up of his days on R&S. (*R&S Records*)

Right: The now-instantly recognisable 'Aphex Grin' appears for the first time on the cover of *...I Care Because You Do*, the third full-length Aphex album. (*Warp Records*)

Left: Per James' bizarre sense of humour, the most abrasive ... *ICBYD* track was issued as the *Ventolin* EP's flagship teaser. (*Warp/Sire/Elektra Records*)

Right: The *Donkey Rhubarb* EP featured James' collaboration with composer Philip Glass and three brand new tracks from the *...ICBYD* sessions. (*Warp Records*)

Left: The artwork for James and µ-Zic's Mike Paradinis collaboration riffs on Milton Bradley board games. (*Rephlex Records*)

Right: Another creepy smile from James adorns his continued foray into drill 'n' bass, the *Richard D. James Album*. (*Warp/Sire Records*)

Left: Children bearing James' face run amok in the 'Come to Daddy' music video. (*Chris Cunningham*)

Right: In the same video, a horrifying demon emerges from a TV to frighten the life out of an innocent bystander. (*Chris Cunningham*)

Left: James cameos in the same video in a grotesque form, reunited with his facially identical children. (*Chris Cunningham*)

Right: Another twisted character from James and Cunningham's imagination can be seen in the lengthy 'Windowlicker' promo. (*Chris Cunningham*)

Left: Parodying the excesses of some gangsta rap videos, James appears in style in his gargantuan limousine. (*Chris Cunningham*)

Right: The 'Windowlicker' girl, later to be paid tribute to in a sketch by renowned Swedish artist H. R. Giger. (*Chris Cunningham*)

Left: The *Girl/Boy* EP is morbidly decorated with an image of James' deceased twin brother's grave. (*Warp/Sire Records*)

Right: The *Come to Daddy* EP shares its entourage of disturbing Aphex children with the title track's video. (*Warp/Sire Records*)

Left: Likewise, a scantily clad woman from the 'Windowlicker' promo graces the cover of its parent EP. (*Warp/Sire Records*)

Right: The last proper Aphex Twin album for thirteen years, *Drukqs* contains almost two hours of alternately mind-bending and beautiful music. (*Warp/Sire Records*)

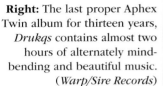

Left: The fake-leather binder given out with the first *Analord* EP was meant to house all eventual eleven entries in the series. (*Rephlex Records*)

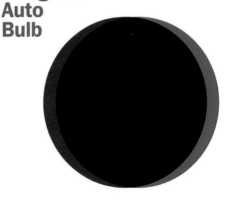

AFX Hangable Auto Bulb

Right: This 2005 compilation of the *Hangable Auto Bulb* EPs cemented James' role in pioneering the drill 'n' bass sound. (*Warp Records*)

Left: James delved deeper into his experimental/modern classical side with this 2012 performance at The Barbican.

Right: At the same concert, James demonstrated his 'Interactive Tuned Feedback Pendulum Array' as shown here.

Left: James gives the thumbs-up at the end of the Barbican performance, as applause rings out.

Right: For his live DJ sets – like this one from Coachella 2019 – James collaborated with designer Weirdcore to create audience-interactive graphics.

Left: The audience dance hypnotised at James' command of tracks old and new at his 2019 Coachella performance.

Right: Intense spirals and patterns flash on screen to signal the chaotic end of James' set at the same show.

The Tuss
"Rushup Edge"
Written & Produced by Karen Tregaskin
Published by Chrysalis
A1: Synthacon 9
B2: Last Rushup 10
www.rephlex.com
Made in England
CAT 189 LP / B

REPHLEX

Left: Although credited to Karen Tregaskin, the Tuss was later revealed to be another side project of James'. (*Rephlex Records*)

CAUSTIC WINDOW

Compilation

Right: The label of the rare *Caustic Window* compilation, which collected tracks from the various EPs James released under that pseudonym. (*Rephlex Records*)

```
APHEX TWIN
SYRO
minipops 67 [source field mix]................120.2
XMAS_EVET10 [thanaton3 mix]...................120
produk 29.....................................101
4 bit 9d api+e+6..............................126.26
180db_........................................130
CIRCLONT6A [syrobonkus mix]...................141.98
fz pseudotimestretch+e+3......................138.85
CIRCLONT14 [shrymoming mix]...................152.97
syro u473t8+e [piezoluminescence mix].........141.98
PAPAT4 [pineal mix]...........................155
s950tx16wasr10 [earth portal mix].............163.97
aisatsana.....................................102
London venue hire for planning meeting
with international team.......................£0.00143
Promotion team in Germany.....................£0.00331
Outdoor postering in Italy....................£0.00066
Refreshments and lunch for promo team
album listening in Paris......................£0.00043
Hotel in Seattle for album playback meeting...£0.00049
Postage costs for US radio promotion mailout..£0.00304
Packing CD and booklet........................£0.06192
Website bandwidth costs.......................£0.00204
Venue and equipment costs for
London listening event........................£0.00163
Online advertising in Norway..................£0.00099
Promotion and marketing team in Norway........£0.00156
Online advertising in Australia...............£0.00338
Promo CDs for US press promotion..............£0.00018
Hotel rooms for international label managers...£0.00311
Promo CDs for US radio promotion..............£0.00184
A2 retail poster for Japan....................£0.00035
Digitisation from tape archive copy of
The Making of Windowlicker....................£0.0009
Refreshments for NYC listening party..........£0.00073
Other online advertising......................£0.01426
Online advertising in Sweden..................£0.00099
Print advertising including
The Fader / Vice and others...................£0.09357
CD-Rs for UK radio promotion..................£0.00035
Small ledger receipts for pre-orders
at independent retail.........................£0.00365
Outdoor postering in Berlin / Cologne /
Hamburg and other cities......................£0.0265
Average distribution charge...................£1.36306
Taxis for planning meeting day in London......£0.00057
Radio advertising in France...................£0.01325
```

APHEX TWIN
SYRO

Left: James' 2014 comeback as Aphex Twin came in various designs: the physical edition cover is presented here. (*Warp Records*)

Right: *Computer Controlled Acoustic Instruments pt2* saw James' continued development with his MIDI composition experiments from *Drukqs*. (*Warp Records*)

```
diskhat ALL prepared1mixed
   13
snar2                        ( WAP375CDD )
     diskhat1
piano un1 arpej
DISKPREPT4
----------
hat 2b 2012b
          disk aud1_12
0035 1-Audio
---
disk prep calrec2 barn dance ( s l o )
DISKPREPT1
----------
diskhat2
piano un10 it happened
     hat5c 0001 rec-4
                 -
```

CHEETAH

Aphex Twin

Left: The retro equipment used on *Cheetah* was echoed by its cover and titular reference to 1980s tech company Cheetah Marketing. (*Warp Records*)

Right: The final 'new' Aphex Twin release to date, the *Collapse* EP, was also the most musically gripping since *Syro*. (*Warp Records*)

Above: Weirdcore was enlisted to create the 'T69 Collapse' video, using AI software to imprint the Aphex logo onto Cornish landscapes. (*Weirdcore*)

Below: As well as these nods to James' home, other various strings of code and languages are spliced through the video. (*Weirdcore*)

Above: The trippy, oscillating effect seen throughout the promo was achieved by using Style Transfer, which blends photos and videos together. (*Weirdcore*)

Below: The video's final minute dives into a colourful wormhole, overlaid with patterns not dissimilar from James' live show graphics. (*Weirdcore*)

Above: James in Moscow in the 1990s.

Below: The genius, Richard David James, himself. (*Martyn Goodacre*)

Album: Richard D. James Album (1996)
Alias: Aphex Twin
Personnel:
Richard D. James: Producer, performer, writer
Release date: November 1996 (UK), January 1997 (US)
Chart placings: UK: 62
Running time: 32:51 (UK); 43:29 (US)
Record label: Warp (UK); Sire (US)

Following the momentary detour of *Expert Knob Twiddlers,* James resumed his exploration into the ever-growing genre of drill-'n'-bass that he helped foster with the pioneering *Hangable Auto Bulb* EPs. Inspired by his collaborators Luke Vibert and Squarepusher – themselves simultaneously pushing the boundaries of electronic music – James refined the sound by going almost completely digital. This allowed him to manipulate sounds and samples more precisely and carefully, meaning they could be as versatile as any traditional synthesizer once fed into the computer.

One of the album's most instantly-captivating parts is the reintroduction of James' classical obsession: last heard on *ICBYD* and its constituent EPs. This time, in contrast, these embellishments take on a more warm and friendly tone than that album's dark reverberated caverns. In 1998, James explained to Ben Thompson for his book *Seven Years of Plenty*, that to create the illusion of a string section, he 'bought a violin for eight quid from a car-boot sale in Dalton, and learnt ... enough to sample'. He then edited these single-note samples, adding multiple layers of violin to create his own digital string section. Crafting the drums was just as – if not more – labour-intensive. To gain the desired effect of time stretching and general skittering, James – egged on by Luke Vibert – worked in incredibly small rhythmic-time intervals, much faster than most drummers could hope to play: sending drum spillages left, right and centre.

Reviews for *Richard D. James Album* (which from here will be referred to as *RDJ Album*) were nearly unanimously positive – it's not surprising when you consider the album combined many of the most-praised Aphex Twin sounds, reshaped into a delightfully new and fresh contortion. *Spin*'s examination pointed out the potential links between the album title, cover and vocal content: '(It) might just be the first electronica LP that not only gropes for narrative, but also aspired to an abstract sort of autobiography', the review claimed, not wholly unreasonably. Due to the far-more-inviting atmosphere (despite the hefty breakbeats), it's James' most melodic work since *SAW 85-92.*

Sadly, the album didn't repeat the comparative success of *SAW Volume II,* and reached only 62 in the UK albums chart. But this hasn't stopped it from becoming a fan favourite. In January 1997, the Sire US version added the previous *Girl/Boy* EP as a bonus. Another arguable *bonus* came with the album's earliest releases containing a plastic sachet filled with a lock of James' hair.

'4' (3:37)

It's difficult to think of a better track to start the album than this. Effectively a three-minute summary of most of the bits and pieces strung throughout the album, '4' wastes no time in showing the hyperactive drum tracks and their surprisingly close relationship with the sombre bed of strings and achingly melancholic synth. Everything has this indescribable nostalgic, wistful edge. The drum fluctuations scratch at the fabric of time, whilst the video-game synths paint alluring and bewitching motifs – their tearjerking potency underlined by the occasional vocal-sample interjections and complete percussive breakdowns. It's an incredibly totemic watermark for the rest of the album.

'Cornish Acid' (2:14)

As the short length may suggest, 'Cornish Acid' is a contrasting and piecemeal offering (to '4' at least). Befitting its name, the 303 bass-synth bubbles intensely under a dissonant pad as the drums simplify just a little to make way for the octave scraping of the bass. Things get more unsettling as it trundles along, with the drums skipping forward and backwards, pulling the stalwart acidic burps along with it into dial-up oblivion.

'Peek 824545201' (3:05)

As unwieldy as the title's string of numbers, this track boasts a head-scratching technicality, increasing in size from the relatively humble structure of 'Cornish Acid'. A watery organ melody submerges the high-definition detail of the programming: pings, sprays and precise blasts all burst out of the speakers without becoming overly flaunted. The continued bare mix just magnifies the invention that can stem from maximising the quality of less rather than settling for an overwhelming quantity of instruments.

'Fingerbib' (3:48)

This is another pinnacle of James' career, making this the second in just four tracks: a testament to this album's enduring quality. The vibrato-soaked melody rides over the crests of the numerous heavenly cascades of synths and strings. With the latter's masterful cushion of sound, it's no surprise that the classical collective Alarm Will Sound decided to cover this track on their orchestrated tribute to James' work. Like '4', 'Fingerbib' (with its childlike portmanteau) mines a path of nostalgic euphoria, which even the piece's momentary corruption can't shatter the illusion of.

The rhythm is disarmingly simple, particularly by James' exacting standards at this point, almost forcing you to take in the sumptuous harmony and examine its sugary bliss even closer. It's another completely masterful expression of naked emotion, the like of which – at least in the Aphex catalogue – we haven't seen since 'Stone in Focus'. It's more than worthy of all the praise it receives.

'Carn Marth' (2:33)

This heavily compressed rhythm marks a sudden return to drill-'n'-bass antics. Following the example of 'Laughable Butane Bob', the track juggles another pure melody with the lightning-speed headbanging that the track's percussive burrows demand. Both are expertly balanced. The former is an echo of a non-existent pop song, brought to extremes by the piece's close, while the latter tunnels through phased goodness, maintaining the runaway-train speed, and even upping the ante with savage, juddering snares and samples.

'To Cure a Weakling Child' (4:03)

As you might've guessed, the 'Weakling Child' is James himself, showing the power of his digital workstation by transforming samples of his own voice. As such, the entire track has a subtle uneasy feeling, acting as the middle ground between the antithetical extremes of the charming and appropriately guileless melody and the bike-chain clicks-and-clacks of the haywire drums. The chirpy and content harmonic aspects hark back to the tranquillity of 'Lichen', and the beat elasticity pulls the rest into even-greater hardcore extremes, sealing it in a layer of spontaneous mischief-making suitable to the exposed innocence of the whole piece.

'Goon Gumpas' (2:02)

This is a display of James' wielding of his sampling system to transform the notes he could realistically play on his secondhand violin, into an entire wall of cavernous strings. Switching between obtrusive *pizzicato* and collected *legato*, the short interlude is coated in reverb, making the distinction between reality and digital processing even less audible. Wobbly synths guide it along to reach its relaxing destination with gusto.

'Yellow Calx' (3:04)

The final entry in the loose 'Calx' trilogy is one of the most transparent and thrilling tracks of any Aphex project. It ties an anticipatory low-bit synth hook soaked in warmth to the almost-*musique concrete* gear shifts and ball-bearing boomerangs of the percussion. Predicating the glitched-up travelogues later to find a home on *Drukqs*, 'Yellow Calx' throws multiple conflicting parts at the listener without becoming needlessly inordinate. Each knotty thicket of beats or notes has a defined purpose, continually propelling everything forward like a racing driver in complete control of their vehicle.

'Girl/Boy Song' (4:52)

In an album stuffed to the brim with awe-inspiring pieces, 'Girl/Boy Song' may just be the most brilliant of them all. The initial sounds of James' digital orchestra tuning up don't prepare the listener at all for the rapturous barrage to follow. The drums are assuredly fleet-footed, and the cymbal hits maintain a continual catharsis in the high end. Meanwhile, the melodies that tiptoe around this artillery-fire heaven are utterly breathtaking. Utilising a host of instruments – from cradling strings to the nursery-rhyme taps of a glockenspiel – James pieces together an electronic symphony of plucked motifs and lapping waves of *pizzicato* cello.

The track – and arguably the entire LP – culminates in all the sky-scraping percussion programming dropping out to let the melodic elements grow into a blissful ensemble expression of liberation and joy. Very few Aphex Twin tracks come close to the unadulterated beauty resonating here. Only adding to the track's quality, is its influence – James' numerous integrations of classical and drill-'n'-bass came to fruition here, leaving their mark on other electronic musicians, like Venetian Snares and hip-hop artists like the venerable Death Grips or Injury Reserve. The track is another phenomenal landmark: there's no other term for it.

'Logan Rock Witch' (3:33)

James closes this very brief album with a self-conscious, goofy track that's not too far removed from 'Next Heap With'. Constructed on a base of cartoonish sound effects and schlock-horror-movie organ, a sinister keyboard riff and a multitude of other percussive segments are layered to maximise the conflict between cheese and anxiety. It's typically destabilising and on the surface, doesn't seem to fit with the rest of the LP, but the track somehow manages to sum up the mischievous attitude that permeates even the album's most serious moments.

The EPs, Part 6: 1996-1999
Girl/Boy (1996)
Alias: Aphex Twin
Personnel:
Richard D. James: Producer, performer
Release date: August 1996
Chart placings: UK: 64
Running time: 15:32 (Original); 21:17 (Website)
Record label: Warp (UK); Sire (US)

Equivalent to *Donkey Rhubarb*'s relationship with *ICBYD*, *Girl/Boy* is a companion EP to the *RDJ Album* – released a few months before it to provide a taster of James' continued ventures into drill 'n' bass. The strongest link comes from the presence of the title track in three different versions (the first confusingly subtitled 'NLS Mix', despite being identical to the album version), and a handful of miscellaneous tracks from the time. The EP has the rare distinction of featuring James on vocals, that are – for the most part – untampered with: most notably on 'Milk Man' and 'Beetles'.

   The cover was a point of discussion at the time, depicting a gravestone bearing the name Richard James. Many journalists said it was a morbid prank by James. But, as it transpired, the gravestone belonged to James' brother (also named Richard) who, sadly, died at birth. He is potentially the sibling indicated by the 'twin' in the Aphex Twin moniker.

'Milk Man' (4:09)
The most fully-realised track on this truncated EP (aside from the original version of the title track) begins with James blankly reciting how he wishes 'the milkman would deliver my milk in the morning'. This somehow turns into James claiming he 'would like some milk from the milkman's wife's tits'. His monotone delivery is placed at odds with the music-box chimes of the instrumentation. Possessing a strong tune, 'Milk Man' is an enjoyable track.

'Inkey$' (1:24)
Pretty much solely a percussion workout, this features some ominous bass dives and prominent ride cymbal. For a track that's so focused on the drums, you'd expect as much thrilling complexity as the programming on the *RDJ Album*, but it's altogether flimsy and surprisingly uninteresting.

'Girl Boy (£18 Snarerush Mix)' (1:57)
As we've come to expect, any Aphex remix is destined to be a whole other track entirely. This variant of 'Girl/Boy Song' marries a downtempo beat to drunken strings and resonant organ before re-entering drill-'n'-bass mode with a snare-dominated loop. It's mostly inconsequential, and eminently forgettable.

'Beetles' (1:31)

'Beetles' is a weird, twisted pop song. Imagine Pink Floyd's Syd Barrett let loose with some synths, and you're probably close to the sound of this track. The constantly-changing pitch and plucky swing underneath is disjointed, yet it slots into the discomforting atmosphere the song plunders: making it a successful experiment. The vocal melody is also strangely catchy, despite its monotony.

'Girl Boy (Redruth Mix)' (1:40)

The 'Girl/Boy Song' remix takes the form of a hyper 303 crashing into the staggered beat, with some much-needed textural variety in the mallet percussion. It only lasts a minute before a processed vocal outro takes its place, so, naturally, it doesn't lead anywhere in particular, though it ends up being more accomplished than the 'Snarerush' mix just by virtue of shake-ups in the timbre department.

Website bonus tracks
'milkman instrumentil' (1:35)

Ignore the botched spelling, and you have an accurate summary of this track. It's a totally instrumental version of 'Milk Man'. Being wordless allows the song to show off its hidden instrumental complexity, but also reminds you how important this track's vocals actually are.

'milkman bonus beets' (1:33)

This is just percussion offcuts from 'Milk Man'. While they don't merit extra listening, they reinforce James' spellbinding way with drums, and the freedom a digital workspace clearly gave him.

'growth inst. (blonder)+6, ru' (2:37)

Somehow this wasn't included in the EP tracklist, which is shocking considering how much more developed the sound is compared to how structurally bony most of the project actually is. The restrained, melancholy melody is as soft as the tempered percussion, making this a better, muted closer to the EP overall.

Come to Daddy (1997)
Alias: Aphex Twin

Personnel:
Richard D. James: Producer, synthesizer, piano, guitar, bass, drum machine, vocals
Release date: October 1997
Chart placings: UK: 36
Running time: 33:25 (Original); 44:19 (Website)
Record label: Warp (UK); Sire (US)

Along with 1999's *Windowlicker, Come to Daddy* is the most-well-known Aphex Twin release, and achieved James' second highest single-chart placement: 36, for the title track. The EP fluctuates between the manic, abrasive drill-'n'-bass he'd spearheaded for the last few years and more typical drum-'n'-bass elements to embellish the nicer tracks.

Aside from the project's popularity, the other notable thing about *Come to Daddy* was it being the first release where video director and artist Chris Cunningham worked with James. Prior to his engagements with James, Cunningham worked with Warp labelmates Autechre on some of their videos in 1996, and also britpop bands The Auteurs and Gene. He'd also been supervisor for the animatronics on Stanley Kubrick's film *A.I. Artificial Intelligence.*

Cunningham and James (and James' usual design company, Designer's Republic) worked together on the EP artwork and video for 'Come to Daddy (Pappy Mix)', uniting them through the terrifying iconography of James' face placed onto many different children. As with most previous Aphex Twin EPs, the video was a surefire contributor to *Come to Daddy*'s success, following similar disturbing clips from artists like Nine Inch Nails ('Closer') and The Prodigy ('Firestarter'). However, it was becoming more difficult to shock the public through the visual arts. That didn't stop Cunningham and James from trying, though – producing a severely disturbing narrative circling around the chilling visages of the 'Aphex children' and a grotesque demon they summoned to wreak havoc on an industrial estate. The hyperreal colour grading and lightning-fast camera movement juxtaposed a fairly typical area against the nightmarish Lynchian antics of a particularly frightening fever dream. The fact that the audio track was originally intended as a parody, says a lot about the ease with which James can craft horrifying scenarios, in music and in video.

The EP was originally issued in two parts, splitting the eight tracks equally, with the second helping released in an orange sleeve to commemorate the usage of 'To Cure a Weakling Child' in an advertisement for Orange telecommunications. The two parts were combined for the CD issue, forming the version found on streaming today.

'Come to Daddy (Pappy Mix)' (4:23)

Originally meant as a jokey death-metal parody, this came to be one of James' most enduring and well-known tracks. Mixing spine-chilling lyrics (made ten times more discomforting by the screamed and grizzled vocal approach common to the gore-infested world of death metal) with jagged, overdriven guitars, added up to the hardest instrumental James had yet come up with.

Retaining the drill-'n'-bass tendencies of the *RDJ Album* but with none of its warmth, 'Come to Daddy' is an abrasive delight that rolls around in its own audio filth sans inhibition. The drums are maniacal at their calmest, and ferocious when let loose over the grinding walls of guitar. Live versions around the time, pushed the track even further into noise with the infamous screaming section (at which point it's scientifically impossible to not headbang) – practically making fun of the existence of the analogue VU-meter red zone, refusing to let the listener breath until the track has relinquished.

'Flim' (2:57)

From unsettling to untampered beauty, the transition from the screeching halt of the 'Pappy Mix' to 'Flim' is complete audio whiplash. Thankfully, being an Aphex Twin fan should prepare you for these sudden changes. Another perennial fan favourite, 'Flim' is a utopian and idyllic sound vision. The rounded drums stay their hand whilst a wistful melody emerges from the gooey sweetness of the airy keys.

Like 'Stone in Focus' or 'Fingerbib', the track plunges headfirst into a blurry representation of nostalgia, and an infant wonder that renders everything as mysterious yet somehow beauteous. The quaint synth decays that bleed pleasurably into one another have clearly stood the test of time – clearly, a forefather to the late-2010s synthwave movement, which had a similar goal of diving headfirst into a not-quite-real place of remembrance.

'Come to Daddy (Little Lord Faulteroy Mix)' (3:48)

The second of three 'Come to Daddy' reworks is totally different to the unhinged metal of the original. Taking on a drunken swagger with keys that sound as if they're struggling to remain upright, the focus is on the eerie voice of a child, presenting in various pitches throughout. The perturbed melody recalls 'Milk Man', and the shuffling drums could've been found on the *Ventolin* EP. But these clear links to other tracks prevent this mix from equalling the first version.

'Bucephalus Bouncing Ball' (5:45)

According to Autechre's Sean Booth (speaking on a forum Q&A), 'Bucephalus Bouncing Ball' was a riposte to the Warp track 'Drane' that used the same distinctive bouncing-ball sound. In response to 'Bucephalus Bouncing Ball', Autechre released the sequel 'Drane2' on their great 1998 album *LP5*. The connotations of the title are proven right by the percussive virtuosity constantly on display here, where the drums imitate the gradual 'exponential delay' of a ball hitting the ground. True to form, James manages to make the track (highlighted by dedication to rhythm rather than melody) seem to fly by, seizing the listener from the get-go, making sure to balance the tricky stereo manoeuvres with moments of ambient calm.

'To Cure a Weakling Child (Contour Regard)' (5:10)

This remix of the *RDJ Album* track keeps most of the original features intact, switching that version's comparative linearity for a preview of the 'Windowlicker's idea of using the entire track as its own instrument.

Following these moments of disarray, the song congeals into a bass-weighted rephrasing of the album version, unearthing the giant low-end presence that the latter interpretation forwent, sacrificing most of the voice samples in the process. The *RDJ* version pips it slightly, but it's a worthy addition to the EP nonetheless.

'Funny Little Man' (3:55)
This is perhaps the EP's weirdest and most-disjointed track – the analogue creepiness blanketing the unrelenting growls and chants of another child's voice, processed through extreme autotuning to become altogether alien. The compressed and almost-*too*-relaxed funk sets up the unnerving contrast that the final disturbing text-to-speech deepens. Making disgusting threats, it unveils the rotten core of the unassuming tune – an unsettling subversion that ultimately makes the rest feel unworthy.

'Come to Daddy (Mummy Mix)' (4:24)
The last 'Come to Daddy' mix is built around innocent and loving samples of James' mother Lorna, commenting on his multitude of synths and keyboards. Her request for a 'snare rush' is duly granted, with the rest of the track nestling into James' then-comfort zone – glitchy noises stopping and starting, uncontrollable drums and walls of distortion.

'IZ-US' (3:03)
Like 'Flim', this captures a tender melody, supported by the cushiony caresses of the bass and satisfying jazz-like ride-cymbal loops. Wavering pads with the timbral quality of woodwinds are another well-deserved addition, complementing the syncopated keys. Ingeniously, James dispatches a drum rhythm that's kindest to the ear here, making it even more of a team player than usual by slotting it directly within the analogue undergrowth rather than surfing the top of the mix with virtuosic power. It's a tranquil beauty, closing a great EP.

Website bonus tracks
'forgotten life path' (2:28)
Very much in the vein of the EP's more-melodic tracks and the tightly-constructed chiptune songs of the *ICBYD* bonuses, 'forgotten life path' uses similar chipper synth patches, mostly with a resonant analogue decay. The beat is understated, as is the main theme that fades in and out, making the track a little anonymous despite its cuteness.

'bank lullaby' (1:49)
Even more hushed than 'forgotten life path', 'bank lullaby' takes on the mantle of sleepy incidental music, containing no drums whatsoever. Instead, decaying synth peals ring out in a pseudo-classical fashion, acting as an

enticing prelude to '28 organ'. The title may be a reference to the old branch of the HSBC bank that James was living in at the time.

'28 organ 1.1 (ru, ec, +9)' (6:40)

A breathtaking multi-part suite consisting of at least three sections, '28 organ' paints an entire emotional story – beginning with an introductory melancholy segment that leads straight into effervescent arpeggios. Lonely leads surface from this sugary cacophony, adding dynamic contrast before everything coalesces for the second time, with the notable addition of throbbing bass giving everything a further sense of drive. Parallel to these changes, the beat alternates based on its surroundings, swapping parts to keep things fresh. Of all the superb segments here, the final section must be the best – rising from muffled pads to a triumphant melody, it's the stuff of movie closing-credits credits, encountering all the catharsis that entails.

Windowlicker (1999)
Alias: Aphex Twin
Personnel:
Richard D. James: Producer, performer
Release date: March 1999
Chart placings: UK: 16
Running time: 16:09 (Original); 23:31 (Website)
Record label: Warp (UK); Siré (US)

After the success of *Come to Daddy*, James took an unprecedented (at least for then) year-long hiatus from releasing any music. Whether this was a deliberate action against his growing popular acclaim or not is up to interpretation. If it was, it didn't do much to diminish the size of his new audience. His next release – 1999's *Windowlicker* EP – became his most successful and enduring project yet.

Teaming-up again with Chris Cunningham to make a video for the title track, they carried over the Hellish iconography of *Come to Daddy*, but this time stuck James' face on numerous women, instead of children. It was the video that garnered the project its lasting notoriety, emphasised upon release by the emergence of more and more promo clips daring to plunder previously forbidden worlds of disturbing and thought-provoking imagery. So, somewhat ironically, as much as the 'Come to Daddy (Pappy Mix)' was intended to be a parody, the 'Windowlicker' video aimed for broad comedy rather than layered social commentary. The four-minute curse-ridden intro played up the sexist stereotypes of gangsta-rap videos to an over-the-top extent. The entire video has an extreme dearth of seriousness, in spite of its images. Of course, the clip's longest parts had every female face morphing into James' trademark grinning visage, and the overtly grisly H. R. Giger-approved features of one woman in particular. (The Swiss artist, best known for his work on Ridley Scott's 1980 horror classic Alien, later drew an image of the scene, titled 'The Windowlickers'). These horrifying scenes – plus the obvious anathema of the curse-ridden intro – led to a daytime ban for the video, MTV only allowing it to be shown in a heavily-censored version that removed most of the opening and the clip's more-grisly portions. However, thanks to Cunningham's expert directing style, the video was nominated for Best Video at the 2000 Brit Awards, somehow losing to Robbie Williams.

All of this – and the perverse, corrupted, catchy title track – propelled *Windowlicker* to the higher echelons of the UK chart, reaching 16 before James pushed Warp to delete the single to prevent it rising to the top ten. But despite this, the worldwide admiration for the track and its video wasn't hindered, and fans from many countries congregated in London to watch the video premiere.

The track itself has proven its worth as an inspiration to artists and even genres across the board – ranging from the subgenre wonky and its main composer Flying Lotus, to the hyperpop experiments of the PC Music label (whose A. G. Cook faithfully covered 'Windowlicker' in 2017). It's no wonder that in 2009, fans voted it the most popular Warp Records track. Its importance seems to grow even today: over 20 years after its release.

'Windowlicker' (6:08)

Essentially presenting six minutes of Aphex Twin in a nutshell, 'Windowlicker' has the honour of being one of James' most poppy offerings, and – adversely – one of his heaviest and most intricate. It's also one of his greatest opuses, in a career stuffed full of them. Beginning with a slowed-down vocal snippet coupled with hints of the melody to come, the track immediately lurches into an impressive slice of drum-programming glory, contorting a sinister and heavily-reverberated beat, and interspersing it with wafers of samples and effects. Then we reach the track's most recognisable part – that distinctive vocal hook, adorned with pornographic moans and yelps (most likely from James) that are spun out into the digital stratosphere. If you listen closely, you can discern James singing the word 'window' repeatedly underneath his pitched harmony. Another left-turn occurs mere minutes after this, moving out of pop terrain momentarily towards a more-spacy middle section filled with accidental notes and guest vocals from James' then-girlfriend Nannou – in the background and in a brief spoken passage where she utters, 'J'aime faire les croquettes des chiens', which translates as 'I like to make dog nuggets'.

Following this, we retreat to the more-poppy section. But unlike its first time through, there's a sense of anticipation, that heightens with a faked crescendo. Finally, everything is let loose as James cranks up the distortion to consume every instrument and blend them into a cathartic tidal wave of sonic terror that bleeds into an atonal drone – almost as if the noise has caused his computer to crash under the stress. It's a fittingly-spent ending to a piece that drains every aspect of James' electronic proficiency, and places them into a pool of untampered genius.

'$\Delta Mi{-}1 = -\alpha\Sigma n{=}1NDi[n][\Sigma\varphi{\in}C[i]Fji[n-1] + Fexti[n{-}1]$' (also known as '**Formula**') (5:47)

Typically referred to as 'Formula' or 'Equation', the incomprehensible mathematical title of this piece is indicative of the contents within. Mired in a bit-crushed fog, the track relays the head-scratching feats of 'Bucephalus Bouncing Ball' into further abstract territory. Most of the uncanny effects arrive as a result of James' use of a program called Metasynth that allowed him to turn images into sounds via a spectrogram.

The meltdown at the track's conclusion is home to one of the most infamous musical 'easter eggs' (i.e. a hidden surprise for those dedicated enough to find it). Part of the 'easter egg' was originally discovered in 2001 on the Chaosmachine blog, alleging James had left a 'demon face' in the spectrogram; but in the summer of that year, a man called Jarmo Niisalo discovered by changing some of the spectrogram's parameters revealed an image of James with his trademark sinister grin.

As a *piece*, it's decidedly left-field. It's really an impressionistic, avant-garde expression with very few antecedents.

'**Nannou**' (4:14)

This is another feat of sound design on an EP riddled with clever moments of soundplay. Dedicated to James' French girlfriend at the time, it uses the quaint conceit of a musical box as a basis for irresistible ear candy. Ingeniously framing the creaks and winding noise of a key turning as the percussive anchor, the natural fast clicking providing an opportunity for Richard to insert his drill-'n'-bass chops again. The tinkling bells playing the melody are just as detailed, maintaining the lovable off-balance nature of a music box while forming an intricate showcase for James' knack for a wistful, un-doctored tune.

Website bonus tracks
'**Windowlicker (End-roll Version)**' (1:02)

This bonus is a version of the short 'Windowlicker' reprise heard over the video credits. It has a pronounced, rubbery beat missing from the original, and a switch between distortion and phaser on the vocals in the first half, and reverb in the second. A curio, but not worth returning to.

'**Windowlicker (Demo Version) (Antibiotics)**' (1:52)

This very early incarnation has nothing in common with the final version, holding a high-pitched, unintelligible vocal. According to the Aphex Twin website, it's saying 'You should not drink and take antibiotics'. There's also a chiming melody that would work on 'Nannou'. This is nowhere close to the quality of the track's final form.

'Windowlicker scratch Intro (cos-mix)' (4:27)

This is just the first four minutes of the video, complete with the rapid-fire swearing and ominous effects that sound as if they've been sampled from 'Formula'. James then adds some scratching to a downtempo hip-hop version of 'Windowlicker', which could've been a cool beat for an MC to rap on. But as a whole, this really only works in the context of the video.

Album: Drukqs (2001)
Alias: Aphex Twin
Personnel:
Richard D. James: Producer, piano, synthesizer, keyboards, harmonium, percussion, programming, treatments, sampler
Release date: October 2001
Chart placings: UK: 22; US: 154
Running time: 100:41 (Original); 116:56 (Website)
Record label: Warp (UK); Sire (US)

Unlike the release strategy of previous records (essentially on a whim, whenever James felt like what he had was good enough to put out), *Drukqs* ended up being somewhat premature. Firstly, an MP3 player belonging to James – containing hundreds of unreleased Aphex Twin and Squarepusher tracks – was accidentally left on a plane. This left these 180 tracks susceptible to leaks on the burgeoning online bootleg community. Moreover, James wanted to fulfil his contract with Warp so he could start a label with Tom Jenkinson (AKA Squarepusher), who – according to James in a contemporary interview with Heiko Hoffmann – said he hated everything on Warp.

As for the album length, its sheer size allowed for James to go on musical excursions that were previously only allocated small roles in the greater overall sound of a release. His modern-classical/electroacoustic side, flourished on *Drukqs*, combining a mixture of gamelan, mallet percussion, solo piano pieces and prepared-piano explorations.

In a post attached to the Soundcloud single 'Diskhat all Prepared1mix (snr2mix)', James explained that on *Drukqs* he used a combination of Yamaha Disklavier and midi-controlled solenoids to perform with the physical instruments. The Disklavier is a piano capable of self-playing, controlled via a computer using MIDI connectivity. This allowed James to compose pieces for piano that would be impossible to play with human hands.

The album's other half is made up of ultra-complex drill-'n'-bass tracks, which are meticulously programmed, and unfold at scathingly fast speeds. They build on the experiments of *Hangable Auto Bulb* and *RDJ Album* by incorporating elements from acid techno, and have longer and more-progressive structures that travel through even-more phases than the former album's longest tracks. Finally, there are a few less-easily-classifiable tracks that are used to break up these two warring styles, mainly circling around field recordings or dark ambience as a method of stark tonal contrast.

It's defiantly eclectic, and is the most varied Aphex Twin album of all, which rubbed many critics the wrong way. In fact, *Drukqs* is the outlier in the mainline chronology, being extremely polarising at the time. Many criticised the album for not improving on prior sounds (strange, considering the widely-praised *Syro* mined older styles much more frequently), and questioned whether its length was necessary. However, in recent years, its stock has increased rapidly, and the album has been solidified as a fan favourite. Its multitude of charms demonstrate James' capability in multiple genres (as if that wasn't transparent enough already), and revealed that his proficiency reached to the acoustic world, without resorting to being ungenuine about these other musical landscapes. It shouldn't be surprising that James can achieve all of this, but the way he deftly presents this variety is still staggering.

'Jynweythek' (Also known as 'Jynweythek Ylow') (2:23)
Starting off on a light note, 'Jynweythek' marks the first instance of James' continuous use of prepared piano on the LP. A wind-up melody much like the one found on 'Nannou' is altered by the metallic edges of the objects placed between the piano strings, bringing the track closer to the microtonal percussion of gamelan music. In another form, the music could pass for pop, but James deliberately serrates the pure edges to – contrary to the drill-'n'-bass ethos – meld the tune and rhythm into a single entity – forming an accomplished, quietly haunting composition in the process.

'Vordhosbn' (4:51)
The differences between the first two tracks area microcosm for the differences threaded throughout the album. 'Vordhosbn' is a, frankly, exhilarating journey, riding the crest of a multi-pronged beat that runs the gamut of techno, drill-'n'-bass and IDM. Ensnared within are several alternately-subdued and expressive melodies coated in church reverb. Coupled with the underwater-like bass stabs, this is a towering synthetic presence to match the rhythm work. A popular fan-made visualiser on YouTube pairs the track with video of a high-speed train – appropriate since even its movement between the dynamic sections never lets the pace drop.

'Kladfvgbung Micshk' (2:06)
The album's sound design is typically stellar, and 'Kladfvgbung Mischk' demonstrates this wonderfully. The muted bass notes and clanking of the prepared piano feel as if they're being played in the same room as the listener, cultivating an oppressive atmosphere through the dissonance. This makes up for the lesser grip of the computer-controlled illusion – using the noises of 'Jynweythek', but foregoing its natural flow.

'Omgyjya-Switch7' (4:52)
This begins with one of the most maniacal beats of any electronic track, and masochistically introduces itself with a combination of distorted whip cracks and the digital meltdown of a snare drum. The purpose is soon revealed, as the rubbery acid synths make a comeback, firing bullet holes into the piece as other motifs ring out into the ether: a bonus display of analogue technology. Three-quarters of the way in, a genuinely delightful analogue

melody is momentarily substituted for the chaos, only for the unhinged percussion to force its way back in, with even-more-strafing trails of feedback to round-out the whirlwind trip.

'Strotha Tynhe' (2:12)

An unsettling piano piece, without any need for prepared objects to bring out the haunted-house atmospherics wrought by the sustain pedal. As soon as any consonant phrases are formed, a dissonant entry rushes in to take its place, giving the composition an air of uncertainty and unpredictability. While not as heartbreaking as 'Nanou2', or as dramatic as 'Kesson Dalek', 'Strotha Tynhe' holds its own as a disconcerting tribute to composers like the great Messiaen, who also balanced the conjunct and disjunct in his work.

'Gwety Mernans' (Also known as 'Gwely Mernans') (5:08)

One of two completely ambient works on *Drukqs*, 'Gwety Mernans' is similar in direction to the barren wastelands aurally depicted on *SAW Volume II*. Tied down by a rotating-blade-type noise panning from left to right, high piano notes circle as ghostly musical figures. All the while, the underpinned sound changes rhythm, never allowing anything to settle in one musical nook. Like the *SAW Volume II* tracks that relied heavily on atmosphere, this track paints a bleak picture of abandonment, delineating some age-old machinery being left to churn for millennia until it just fades into nothingness – as the tremolo noise does, leaving only echoes behind as proof of its existence.

'Bbydhyonchord' (2:33)

Following one of the least-harmonic tracks, comes 'Bbydhyonchord', full to the brim with charming motifs played on vintage analogue gear for that extra-cushiony feel. The bongo rhythm is a reminder of the role repetition played in older forms of electronic music, which this track does a fantastic job of replicating. In fact, the quiet in general, reinforces the greater terracing of dynamics maintained throughout the LP, setting up for the thrill ride of 'Cock / Ver10', while standing unassuming as a heartwarming representation of the synth pop that populated James' childhood.

'Cock / ver10' (5:18)

This is another mind-bending foray into drum-'n'-bass, assimilating the acidic textures of 'Bbydhyonchord', and spitting them out in mangled, ferrous forms. Some of the analogue synths from 'Omgyjya-Switch7' return, gliding serenely over the pinball-energy backdrop. A yell of 'Come on you c***s, let's have some Aphex acid!', opens a tunnel into factory-floor soundscaping – the quiet before the 303 storm rages; no synth-pad solitude in sight. Like all the lengthy tracks here, this parades through numerous fantastically-delirious phases without a slip-up in sight. Even aside from the showstopping top elements, in this track – and the others – there are ongoing edits underneath, giving us a momentary glimpse into the intertwining musical cogs that work tirelessly to improve the thrill of the auditory experience.

'Avril 14th' (2:05)

This track is James' most-played track on streaming services and remains the most-well-known composition from his large body of work. Surely this is partly down to the piece's arresting beauty – the closest James has come to the études and piano sonatas of the romantic composers. The grouping of the frail upper register with the walking bass line is ingeniously simple, but results in sombre but spectacular harmonies and links across the piano. Once you add the spellbinding main motif, you have a powerful miniature that's still the champion of all the album's (admittedly very good) electroacoustic tracks.

But, of course, the elephant in the room is Kanye West's sampling of the track in his 2010 song 'Blame Game' from his album *My Beautiful Dark Twisted Fantasy*. West uses the latter half as the basis. But it wasn't the context that was the problem. James has claimed that the handling of his sample was bordering on plagiarism, with his helpful approach rebuffed by West's team, who apparently said the sample is 'not yours, it's ours'. As would be expected, this exchange left a bad taste in everyone's mouth, despite 'Richard James' being credited in the album liner notes – indicating the possibility of compensation for the sample.

'Mt Saint Michel + St Michaels Mount' (8:10)

Wasting no time, this hammers straight into its ultra-fast drill-'n'-bass zone, trails of dissonant acid synths bouncing between the chastising regularity and palpable interplay of the kick drum and bass. As an endurance test, it's certainly challenging, even for a drum-'n'-bass fan. But not to worry, because next in the series of miniature movements comes a windswept synth, which drags an immaculately-produced micro-house beat – naturally, turned up to 11 – and breathy vocal snippets that instantly hark back to the melodies of 'Xtal'. These gently coax the track down a different path than its initial promises, presumably drifting over to the 'St. Michaels Mount' portion of the track, and opening the gateway to some heavenly editing tricks that expose further motifs: like peeling an onion. But the final minute delves into utterly-face-melting territory, using the digital studio as an instrument of its own, sending the track through an all-encompassing tremolo effect, until you start to feel nauseous thanks to the barrage of negative space replacing the previously relentless detail. It's absolutely spellbinding.

'Gwarek2' (6:46)

This is an exploration into pure ambience and electroacoustic experimentation, the likes of which we haven't really heard since 'Spots' from *SAW Volume II*. It feels closer to the avant-garde modern-creative jazz of Anthony Braxton than electronica. The combination of tinkling metallic-percussion rolls, faded dark ambient pads and splotches of found sound, birth a spare and despondent environment that threatens to build to an industrial-noise climax at certain points. While the sheer ballsiness of sticking such an unorthodox piece in the middle of an album is commendable, it nearly kills the pacing, diminishing its intended impact.

'Orban Eq Trx 4' (1:35)

A low-slung groove recalling 'Cow Cud is a Twin' is the meat of this track. Actually, aside from a four-note bass ostinato, it's the only musical element. Therefore, while it could plausibly make a fine base for a hip-hop instrumental, on its own, it desperately lacks the qualities needed to help it transcend the status of interlude.

'Aussois' (0:13)

An unintelligible eight-second voice sample dipped in reverb, that serves little-to-no purpose.

'Hy a Scullyas lyf Adhagrow' (2:14)

Another gamelan-influenced, prepared-piano piece along the same melodic lines as 'Jynweythek', punching out a childlike motif that's subsequently deepened by the use of unison and contrary motion in the keyboard phrasing. The bass part juggles chords and arpeggios, while the top end outlines some plucky harmonics, ticking all the boxes in terms of late 18th century Classical composition. It's a well-done pastiche, doing a lot more than 'Orban Eq Trx 4' did in much less time.

'Kesson Dalek' (Also known as 'Kesson Dalef' or 'Kesson Daslef') (1:21)

This is disc one's best solo-piano piece (along with 'Avril 14th'), closing the album's first half in disorienting and elegantly-menacing fashion. With variations on a cascading theme separating flurries of chromaticism with broken chords, it reverts to the Aphex maxim of the disruption of beauty – thus, it fashions a bond between James' musical identity and the piano style of older composers, completing this welding of approaches in as seamless a way as 'Avril 14th', with the addition of a darker element, to garnish.

'54 Cymru Beats' (6:06)

A kaleidoscopic array of sound effects provides the skeletal frame for this busy track. The title might as well refer to the number of minute samples since there's a whole host of them dotted about the piece. In typical Aphex fashion, these disparate snippets are stitched together into an impressive patchwork design, framed by the laser-fire of the bass and rhythmic source code constantly in a state of corruption. Instead of following in the footsteps of the other long tracks here, it focusses on its capacity to bludgeon, with measly morsels of melody left to tidy up any bare sections. As such, it shakes up the (guaranteed chalk and cheese) structure the album has fallen into at this halfway mark, pushing the listener into this overwhelming spectacle with riveting results.

'Btoum-Roumada' (1:58)

Another classical pastiche, this time aiming for a plagal composition, and it completely succeeds. Most of that success is indebted to the choice of instrument. The meditative reverb-smothered bells have an instant grandeur and size that places the listener directly in a church environment, where the *amen* cadences can be realised to their fullest potential. Moreover, the length of the room reverb leads to new tones and sounds being created in a chord or note's aftermath, giving the impression of the lingering perfect harmony birthing a shadow counterpart: highlighting the spellbinding resolutions.

'Lornaderek' (0:31)

The album's most worthwhile non-musical interlude presents a voicemail recording of James' parents (the title portmanteau) wishing him a happy 28th birthday. It's a heartwarming and brief insight into James' life, reminding us of his want to distance himself from the hidden personas so many electronic musicians inhabit.

'QKThr' (Also known as 'Penty Harmonium') (1:27)

Sustaining the beauty of the last two tracks, 'QKThr' sees another instrument added to James' arsenal: the harmonium. Most-readily-associated with the bleak solo work of Nico in a more-modern context, here James plays a forlorn number that ekes out the lonesome atmospherics of his purely-ambient pieces, slotting their careful abstractions over a winsome motif. The extra details of the instrument's creaking tone, purposefully add another layer of gorgeous humanity to an already touching work.

'Meltphace 6' (6:24)

This is a companion to '54 Cymru Beats'. Rather than having a meticulously-considered rhythm section, the track siphons melody from every corner, whether that's the decaying pads or the dial-up synths that burble adjacent to the feathery keys recalling the plagal atmosphere of 'Btoum-Roumada'. In a sense, the track becomes even more important within a wider context, given that this dense melodious approach is the foundation for the rest of James' work, with its restless creativity seemingly unfolding live. There are too many examples to list, but the artillery-fire vocal and drum editing near the end, and the gradual foregrounding of the classical elements, are two of the best, enlivening an already active track.

'Bit 4' (0:25)

A sequel to *Hangable Auto Bulb*'s 'Bit' that's near-identical to that predecessor

– a harsh tone that may have come from the speeding up of one of the album's many tracks.

'Prep Gwarlek 3b' (1:19)

A precursor to the experiments on 2015's *Computer Controlled Acoustic Instruments Pt. 2* EP (*Drukqs* being part 1, naturally), 'Prep Gwarlek 3b' is fixed on rhythm. Even the piano is prepared and oscillates across a dissonant interval. Like 'Kladfvgbung Micshk', the production assists the stifling percussion, with the piano bass notes uncomfortably close, with the mallet instruments sidelined to keep the rigid tempo. Also, like 'Kladfvgbung Micshk', it's not as successful as its spiritual partner (in this case 'Gwarek2').

'Father' (0:57)

Barely a minute long, this almost formless piano piece was titled because James' father apparently liked it. Once again, taking – at least indirect – inspiration from Messiaen, the composition captures little more than a moment of discordancy; the jabs of the keys echoing the harsh intervals played to seem random. It's many people's least-favourite track on the LP, but for me, it acts as a further extension of James' trip through western-classical history, and is important, at least in that contextual regard.

'Taking Control' (7:14)

Starting with what sounds like a LinnDrum rhythm (more '80s nostalgia?), 'Taking Control' is James' sound-manipulation masterclass. Befitting the dystopian lyrical content, it's the most disharmonious epic. Sometimes the trebly synth ripples merge into a noisy gloop underneath the panicked vocal samples (again of Lorna James). The rest of the instrumentation responds to these signifiers, upping the excitement with faster kick-drum rhythms or watery synth textures: to refer to two instances. The track ends with the eerie melodicism seeming to point towards the ascension of the machines, effectively taking over to demonstrate their power.

'Petatil Cx Htdui' (2:11)

This is a piano work that lives in the sea of its own reverb, the breadth of which cannot mask the exquisite handling of – you guessed it – melody. The high-end keyboard use is especially stunning – the minor shapes verging into jazz chord extensions. But perhaps this link isn't so surprising, considering the piece inhabits an impressionistic, wayward post-bop location, and also shows the gentle style of Keith Jarrett's improvisations on the *Sun Bear Concerts*.

'Ruglen Holon' (1:49)

The abrasive chimes of the prepared piano, rear their head again. But this track is more focussed on space than the central instrument. Containing a few brief variations on one motif, a quarter of its length is quiet, perhaps acknowledging its intention to differ from the other prepared pieces, and also recognise the aural battering to ensue on 'Afx237 v.7' and 'Ziggomatic 17'.

'Afx237 v.7' (4:23)

Better known as the soundtrack to Chris Cunningham's short film *Rubber Johnny*, this track is as malleable and, well, rubbery, as would be required for the elastic protagonist to dart about to. With a beat that almost swings in parts, staircases of supple synths cling to each other, reaching new heights of chiptune-inflected mayhem, working in tandem with the drums, for maximum mayhem. The almost-comical and over-the-top layering of the gigantic synth chords and the careering refrain, tells you all you need to know about the dark humour inherent in the knowing disorder of both the track and the short film that goes with it.

'Ziggomatic 17' (8:35)

The LP's final drill-'n'-bass monument is – fittingly – the longest, providing the last energetic peak before slowing down with the closing two songs. Here, James pulls out all the stops to impress all that have made it thus far, giving the listener the definitive overview of the extravagant instrumental style gradually built-up throughout the record. The first quarter is populated by soapy strings of acid synth and an exhilarating drum break, distorting the edges of the mix with its potency and strength. Quieter percussion strains tickle the eardrums, accompanying the bass' slow rise to the driving seat, assuming control and veering into mystifying steel drum sounds and invigorating programming. Although the melody isn't as direct as that of 'Mt Saint Michel...', the chirpy, melancholy finale ranks among the album's most beautiful moments. At the end, we even get a thanks from a computerised Richard: 'Thank you for your attention. Bye'.

'Beskhu3epnm' (2:10)

This comedown is more chilly than the preceding track, but a lot more tranquil. It's pleasant enough, despite the charm of the prepared-piano formula wearing off. Everything seems very distant, managing the dynamics until the clave-type rhythm enters just before the halfway mark. It's not the track's fault that it soon becomes forgettable – unfortunately, its position in the tracklist puts it between not only two of the album's highlights, but staples of James' entire oeuvre.

'Nanou2' (3:25)

You'd think that after 30 tracks, James would've run out of ideas altogether, let alone good ones, but you'd be very much wrong, as 'Nanou2' is one of the five greatest achievements in the Aphex Twin discography. Don't let its relative simplicity throw you off. Every lingering chord radiates absolute melancholy and sadness, with nothing being out of place or unnecessary at any point. It helps that the chords are absolutely divine, the upper-register embellishments helping further poignancy to leak from each musical pore. It's the finest integration of natural decay and silence this side of Talk Talk's *Laughing Stock*.

Judging by the title, the track follows 'Nannou' from *Windowlicker*, but that track's innocence is replaced with an aching sense of loss – perhaps James' expression of the state of his and Nannou's relationship at that time. As a conclusion to such a long album, it may initially seem anticlimactic or too *soft* to seem like a worthy payoff. But with repeated listens, it becomes the only plausible ending, leaving the album on a deliberately sombre note that could indicate conclusion, potential for the future, or neither. And that dichotomy is what makes James' music so fascinating in the first place.

Website bonus tracks
'dRuQks Prepared uN 1' (3:01)
According to the note on the Aphex Twin website, this track was recorded at the bank James lived in for a period of time, and was composed using his first Yamaha Disklavier. It's odd that this textured piece didn't make the cut for the sprawling *Drukqs* – compared to some of the other prepared pieces, it contains a lot more instrumental depth and change throughout, with prepared-piano and percussion trading-off against each other. It's probably the closest James has come to sounding like Tom Waits, at least.

'avril 14th half speed alternative version (re-recorded 2009 Nagra)' (5:07)
The title says it all. Mainly due to the dexterity of the original composition, the track doesn't succumb to being boring or lacking the original's beauty. Rather, the slowed-down approach intensifies the overwhelming warmth; the sonorous texture of the keys, nurturing the soft chords as they ring out gracefully.

'avril 14th reversed music not audio (re-recorded 2009 Nagra)' (2:12)
Another alternate version of 'Avril 14th', recorded at the same time as the half-speed version. This time, the original tempo is kept, but reversed. The piece is actually performed backwards rather than reversed in the production stage, so while it retains some of the album version's most recognisable aspects, it also feels like its own distinct entity.

'Mangle 11' (5:55)
This is the lost progressive drill-'n'-bass track, incorporating elements from its hyperactive album contemporaries, with the notable addition of a more prominent *amen break* to draw closer parallels to drum-'n'-bass. Inevitably, the foregrounding of this well-known beat, dates it more than the album

tracks. Thankfully, the giant-sounding synths and vocal samples in the second half, reinvigorate it, giving way to some truly astounding drum manipulation as it staggers to a close.

The EPs, Part 7: 2001-2007

Drukqs 2 Track Promo (2001)

Alias: Aphex Twin

Personnel:

Richard D. James: Performer

Release date: August 2001

Chart placings: Did not chart

Running time: 11:09

Record label: Warp Records

A promo CD containing two remixes of tracks from *Drukqs*, issued in a clear case with an added sticker showing the track titles, which are two of the album's most complex progressive drill-'n'-bass pieces.

'54 Cymru Beats (Argonaut Mix)' (6:02)

As usual, these purported remixes are not what they seem. They cleave so close to the originals, that they might as well be the album versions. Even with deeper listening, barely any changes can be detected. It seems like this version of 'Cymru Beats' is essentially a copy of the album take.

'Cock 10 (Delco Freedom Mix)' (5:07)

With a few more perceptible differences – most obviously, a much greater mix presence of the churning acid bass – this version of 'Cock / Ver10' is a more- worthwhile listen than the prior track. This doesn't stop it being weaker than the album cut – the additions being the source of the problem, by removing some of the LP version's intricate subtlety.

Smojphace (2003)

Alias: Aphex Twin

Personnel:

Richard D. James: Performer, remixer

The Bug, Daddy Freddy: Performers

Producers: Richard D. James; The Bug ('Run the Place Red (AFX Mix)')

Release date: June 2003

Chart placings: Did not chart

Running time: 16:13

Record label: MEN Records

A contrasting EP, released on MEN: a subsidiary label to James' Rephlex. It sees him take on two styles incorporated into his music often, though not usually with this much focus. On 'Run the Place Red (AFX Mix)', James remixes a raggacore track by The Bug, with vocals by Daddy Freddy, while the remaining two tracks are completely noise-based. The CD issue was of note, as it contained an all-black CD: even on the side where the disc is read.

'Run the Place Red (AFX Mix)' (5:06) (James, The Bug, Daddy Freddy)
This is a one-of-a-kind track in the Aphex catalogue since it delves into Raggacore: a melding of drum-'n'-bass and electronic ragga. James injects a healthy serving of *amen-break* chaos, allowing the beat to slide over Daddy Freddy's toasting and singing. The sub-bass – courtesy of The Bug – has an appropriately dub-like weight. All in all, it's a successful experiment, making it a shame that James didn't dip his toes into ragga more often.

'KTPA1' (7:29)
The genre switch-up was teased at the end of the previous track, with bursts of static interrupting the mix. But *this* is a full-on dive into harsh noise. It's the first time James has focussed solely on noise in his music, and perhaps that was for the best. As power electronics and harsh noise stands, this is one of the lesser examples, never really deciding what approach it wants to take. The thin sound at points diminishes its intended powers; as a studio concoction, it just doesn't work that well.

'KTPA2' (3:37)
A shorter noise track that covers similar bases to the first 'KTPA' instalment, intent on corrupting static into small sound bites throughout. As it's shorter than its predecessor, it has a bit more focus and bone-shaking force overall. James' noise experiments come off a lot better in a live setting. Not only does he regularly end his DJ sets in a flurry of improvised noise, but in 2003, he opened for Bjork – as DJ Smojphace – playing nearly two hours of tracks like this to an increasingly-disgruntled crowd.

Analord (2004-2005)
Alias: Aphex Twin (Analord 10); AFX (Analord 1-9, 11)
Personnel (All EPs):
Richard D. James: Producer, performer
Release date: December 2004 – June 2005
Chart placings: Did not chart
Total running time: 3:24:04; 4:36:00 (with 2009 Rephlex-exclusive bonus tracks)
Record label: Rephlex Records

The 11-volume *Analord* series (with the first confusingly numbered as the 10th instalment) was a six-month-long release schedule of low-profile EPs, all created with analogue gear. After the mammoth undertaking that was *Drukqs*, James made sure to stay out of the spotlight for the next 13 years – the most noteworthy release between 2001 and 2004 being the 2003 remix compilation *26 Mixes for Cash*. However, despite the Aphex Twin name being mostly inactive during this time, James was far from lazy, prioritising the rehabilitation of his dormant side-project AFX, and creating a new parallel identity as The Tuss.

And he didn't shy away from larger projects. *Analord* was almost three and a half hours of material. In 2009, Rephlex released 21 more tracks that had been left off the other projects, showing James' continued incredible work ethic, even on such primarily-low-key releases. The majority of the EPs are credited to AFX, but the flagship release *Analord 10,* was attributed to the main Aphex Twin moniker. It was initially sold online via Rephlex, and came with an empty binder with dedicated sleeves to hold the forthcoming EPs (with the Aphex Twin logo on the cover for the first time since *SAW Volume II*).

Arguably, *Analord* was most important for reintroducing James' love of vintage analogue gear. On *Drukqs*, their usage had begun to increase, but it was these 11 EPs that allowed James to make them the star of the show. His arsenal included the Roland TR-606, 808 and 909 for drums; the Roland MC-4 sequencer, and the Roland TB-303 for that classic acid-bass sound. Some tracks were named after the instrument used on them – a classic example being *Analord 10*'s 'Fenix Funk 5', which uses the Synton Fenix Modular synth. This re-embracing of older electronic styles proved to be influential on his musical direction into the 2010s.

In 2006, James released *Chosen Lords* – a condensed compilation of handpicked favourites from the sessions. Unlike the vinyl-exclusive nature of the rest of the series, *Chosen Lords* was released on CD and acted as a useful primer for the other EPs, or as a stand-alone album for those daunted by the length of the full series.

Analord 10 (2004)

Release date: December 2004
Running time: 13:04

'Fenix Funk 5' (5:06)

We launch straight into analogue heaven on 'Fenix Funk 5' – synth wind chimes giving way to woozy vocoder and a downright-dirty bass groove. As we'll see with most of the *Analord* tracks, the drums have that quintessential aged sound, inviting intriguing contrasts with the fleet-fingered programming James' instils. And what a way to introduce the series this is – it's unbelievably funky, touched by spacious flute-like keys that invite a disarming pastoral aura into the multifaceted cushions of sticky sound.

'XMD 5a' (7:58)

Metallic stacks of synth, fade-in in the opening moments, before allowing another off-kilter funk bounce to intervene. The casual ambience isn't all lost, though, with stray, interjecting piano notes wandering into the thick blankets of keys. The first instance of the 303 on the EP, occurs here – spitting out sour lines as the piano enters the spotlight. At the close, a gigantic miasma of synths rises from the ether, drawing the track to an intense conclusion.

Analord 01 (2005)
Release date: January 2005
Running time: 21:57; 26:09 (with 2009 bonus tracks)

'Steppingfilter 101' (4:45)
Though the beginning echoed claps hint at something more sinister, 'Steppingfilter 101' winds its way to being a sweet, melodic track, courtesy of the delightfully-tasteful mix and foamy 303. Any concerns about the drums taking a back seat, are made up for by the liquid drawls of that inimitable Roland bass, especially when they introduce new polyrhythms over the synth-pad cycles near the finish.

'Canticle Drawl' (1:45)
Less fleshed-out, and more like Richard sorting through his bass presets, 'Canticle Drawl' is engulfed almost immediately by a hefty wad of low-end outlining a spare, ascending motif. A few sound changes later, and we're back where we started, the lowest oscillations gaining momentum from the strict rhythm just as the track stops.

'MC-4 Acid' (3:47)
Named after the Roland Micro-Composer sequencer that sometimes took the form of a calculator, 'MC-4 Acid' is a relatively straightforward piece of acid techno, replete with 303 and a smooth, woodblock-heavy drum rhythm. There's little to make it stand out from his multiple other acid tracks, except perhaps for the supple percussion breakdown halfway through. Nonetheless, it's still immaculately produced: like most of the *Analord* offerings.

'Bubble 'n' Squeek 2' (1:31)
Originally unlisted on the EP, this slender track continues where 'MC-4 Acid' left off, adding some gorgeous, airy synth pads underneath the tremors of the stringy acid keyboard. On its own, it's annoyingly meagre, but it does bear some resemblance to the 'Old SAW-era track' (a great unreleased number) that James played live at Field Day 2017.

'Where's Your Girlfriend?' (5:06)
The title's confrontational bent is reflected in the cut-glass sprays of 303 and high-pitched synth, as a prominent drum loop percolates underneath. Things soon get even tenser – the keys begin to distort and change shape alongside a tinny arpeggio: magnifying the well-proportioned drama. A highlight.

'Grumpy Acid' (3:21)

This title foreshadows the uncomfortable 303 wailing above the moody bass and pulsing arpeggios. Intent on crafting a tangled series of loops, the track piles cyclical instrument samples on top of each other to build an even-more-entangled heap of rotating noises. Despite the ending outstaying its welcome, it's another fine track.

'Analord 158b' (1:40)

Basically, a summation of the EP's general sound, 'Analord 158b' isn't the finest of closers, or tracks for that matter. But in the context, it does a good job of wrapping up the sine-wave-loaded contents of the prior tracks. But outside of this specific environment, the less-than-memorable composition can easily be thrown to the wayside, as over-saturation begins to set in.

2009 bonus tracks
'Canticle Drawl (Alternate Version)' (0:36)

Of even less substance than the already-skinny original, this may as well be named 'Pointless', as the blink-and-you'll-miss-it synth herein is just that.

'Where's Your Girlfriend? (Another Version)' (3:36)

A marginally different variant of one of the EP's standout tracks that prioritises its least interesting and engaging elements (the bass and drums) over the majority of the arpeggiated glory the final version presented in spades.

Analord 02 (2005)

Release date: January 2005
Running time: 23:11; 26:43 (with 2009 bonus track)

'Phonatacid' (9:47)

Setting a precedent for this third entry in the series, 'Phonatacid' is a slice of languid funk, filled to the brim with creamy synths and bass bubbles. Immediately we can hear the development of the *Cheetah* sound in-progress. A four-on-the-floor drum rhythm anchors the piece, whilst decaying electronics and stray shards of vocoder stretch out amongst it. It's a high watermark for the collection, sounding vintage and futuristic all at once.

'Laricheard' (2:15)

Tracing the footsteps of 'Phonatacid', 'Laricheard' possesses a soft techno beat over which glaciers of synth pads melt into a pleasing mush. Chorus-laden bass lines oscillate in a syncopated fashion, smoothing off any remaining rough edges, to find a relaxing sweet spot that's rapidly cut off.

'Pissed Up in SE1' (5:14)

Reminiscent of 'If It Really Is Me' from *Surfing on Sine Waves* (mostly due to the warm clicking of the drum machine), 'Pissed Up in SE1' (SE1 is a London postcode) attempts to represent the state of its title through a cocktail of stately melodies roughened-up by the bite of the old synths.

There's some fantastic interplay between the deep-house bass line and the groggy treble keys, capturing an unsteady, sickly feeling perfectly throughout.

'Bwoon Dub' (5:55)

The bass is where this track is really at. Chest-thumping slabs of dubby goodness resonate through the dirty bass lines and the straightforward drum beat. The melodic synths also hark back to dub roots, play-acting as melodicas in the background. It suffers from its length, but – to its credit – it cultivates a thunderous atmosphere while it's around.

2009 bonus track
'Carnival Acid' (3:32)

I'm glad this was left as a bonus track, as it doesn't mesh with the EP's more-relaxed style. For what it is – a basic piece of Aphex acid with a nervy melody line straight from an early synth-pop record – it's serviceable but is by far the weakest of the bunch here. But the track is spot on, texturally: a strength felt throughout the entire project.

Analord 03 (2005)

Release date: February 2005
Running time: 18:44; 23:24 (with 2009 bonus track)

'Boxing Day' (6:36)

Spiralling out into a surge of sparkly sounds, 'Boxing Day' begins with the neon glow of an arpeggiator – the foundation on which the tempered extraneous features are built on. Their jagged edges are managed by the calm somnambulance of the external pads and the unblemished attacks of acid bass.

James is canny enough to switch the instrumental focus too, preventing the grating feeling that graced his earlier work.

'Midievil Rave 1' (2:44)

The title's pun on 'medieval' doesn't really ring true, but the 'evil' part definitely does. Restless three-note-or-less arpeggios poke their heads above ground regularly, as if this rave is constantly interrupted at every turn. I'm almost certain it was created to be deliberately ugly since that's probably the sole aspect in which it succeeds.

'Klopjob' (5:24)

Commencing with an almost triumphant chord progression redolent of Orbital, 'Klopjob' is another oddity. The 303 conducts its usual spidery reach, as the beat – which has a lot in common with James' early percussion tracks – and blocks of synth intertwine to unmask their free-flowing union. By the last minute or so, it's stripped to its barest essentials, permitting the 303 to run wild over the condensed backing.

'Midievil Rave 2' (4:00)

Reappropriating the stop/start antics of its numerical predecessor, 'Midievil Rave 2' adds more flesh to the original skeleton. A fat bass line plays in unison with those repeated motifs, but – thankfully – a buoyant lead takes over to distribute some improvisational variety. Despite having the hereditary traits of 'Midievil Rave 1', this sequel at least tries to improve and fill out its subject – and it is commendable for that.

2009 bonus track
'Stabbij' (4:21)

There's a strain of deep-house influence resonating through this, particularly showcased in the slippery sliding bass line doing most of the heavy lifting. In comparison, the beat isn't that danceable, thanks to the multitude of effects piled on top of it. Half the time, it's missing from the broth of tremolo synths around it. It's a very nice track, and one that could have surely taken the place of 'Midievil Rave 1'.

Analord 04 (2005)

Release date: March 2005
Running time: 18:25; 31:04 (with 2009 bonus tracks)

'Crying in Your Face' (4:25)

Driving forward with one of the most emotionally-charged 303 performances on any *Analord* EP, 'Crying in Your Face' runs with its minor-key chord progression and theme; spectral notes floating in and out as it dips further into ghostliness. A vocoder emits indecipherable words, which is appropriate – the track's modus operandi is prioritising feeling, felt directly as it slips into a mournful, ambient coda, dissipating beautifully at the piece's climax.

'Home Made Polysynth' (4:07)

Snug and warm is the primary feeling radiated from the dulled sirens of the synth pads (presumably homemade), with even the 303 being reined-in to slot into the wider atmosphere. Like 'Crying in Your Face', this track is mostly about the latter. The cosy synths melt together, trading-in long-lasting melodic impact for a more textural bent.

'Halibut Acid' (6:07)

This is a fantastic example of synergy between instruments. Nothing is out of place or taking up too much of the listener's attention. This crucial factor lets the track handle its tried-and-true formula with an eye for intricacy – whether it's the cold syncopated keys or the enticing throwback drum machine, they all serve to benefit each other's positions to maximise the bliss they can emit.

'Breath March' (3:46)

For once in this series, the drums take major pride-of-place, tapping out a scratchy, pinpointed rhythm, while being smothered with the indications of sub-bass and wavering keys. The latter elements are reduced to mere window-dressing – emphasising the unfinished feel running through the track's bare chug.

2009 bonus tracks
'Flutternozzle' (6:28)

Structured like a milder version of James' hardcore techno tracks, 'Flutternozzle' dispatches with an anonymous drum pattern and runny loops with a notably-thin bass presence. A few modular sound effects are added in the hope of sticking, but the sub-par mixing holds everything back from gelling.

'In the Maze Park' (1:31)

This robust and melodic slice of electronica brings back those chiptune synths from '28 organ', and plunges intermittently into precarious territory by reversing and stopping. It's quite gimmicky but harmless enough and deserving of bonus-track status.

'Halibut Acid (Orig. Mix)' (4:35)

This alternate mix of 'Halibut Acid' contains the same essential moving parts as the EP version, but rearranged and traded in and out more often than its EP counterpart. The final release is a comparatively-more-honed and focussed piece of work; the stop/start flirtations here dampening the pacing, while the different aspects have less time to properly interact with each other than they do on the spruced-up final mix.

Analord 05 (2005)

Release date: March 2005
Running time: 10:44; 20:17 (with 2009 bonus tracks)

'Reunion 2' (5:10)

A wobbly choir of synths heralds the calm-before-the-storm that soon enters. Gating and tremolo effects – once paired with a motorik beat – revel in their unbalanced state, enhancing the silkiness of the remaining instrumentation. Even the stalwart components soon destabilise, untethering themselves as a smooth helping of bass slides in to help stomach this hurried madness.

'Cilonen' (5:34)

Coming back to Earth, 'Cilonen' transplants the basic parts of the prior track without the spontaneity of its effects. Instead, it resorts to a more-structured approach – bolting the default puzzle pieces together that sometimes bleed into a gooey melting-pot of sublime synth action – but is hampered by its ability to really take off.

2009 bonus tracks

'Gong Acid' (3:05)

Wrong-footing us right off the bat with the gong hits revealed to be syncopated instead of on the beat, this shares a single melody between duelling 303s in each stereo channel. Running with the slow-buildup form we've been exposed to before, there are ultimately not enough features to truly distinguish the track.

'Reunion 2 (Alt. Version)' (6:23)

Turning the level of palpable havoc up by a few more notches, this alternative 'Reunion 2' brings us forward in time by sprinkling traces of a breakbeat into the mix. Evidently more-claustrophobic than the first time we heard it (everything is louder), the mystery of the final version is sidelined for a more-gaudy take that misconstrues its aims.

Analord 06 (2005)

Release date: April 2005
Running time: 23:00; 37:19 (with 2009 bonus tracks)

'Batine Acid' (5:30)

Grabbing the listener straight away with an elastic bass line, 'Batine Acid' is a solid start to this seventh EP. The enjoyment mostly stems from the chemistry between the two layers of 303, effectively tackling two integral parts of the track at once. Though there's less surprise this far into the sequence, the track still consolidates its strengths.

'Snivel Chew' (4:05)

Zigzagging across the mix is another bout of double-303 goodness, with a portamento-infused pad inserted for good measure. But drum-wise, this track loses points since there's little difference between this clap-infested rhythm and the 'Batine Acid' backing. Still, the linking of melodic elements is as hypnotic as ever: polishing the piece's finish slightly.

'I'm Self Employed' (4:16)
The accomplishment dripping from the title, leads to one of James' most celebratory pieces. The percussion has little difference to the previous two tracks, sadly. But, the ostinati above – soaked in timeworn delay and detuning, for that extra nostalgic kick – are plaintively gorgeous. It's a comforting transmission, not only in the sound's enveloping warmth but in refreshing us of James' knack for standout performances.

'2 Analogue Talks' (1:45)
Recalling the mono experiments of *Analogue Bubblebath 3*, these two interstitial numbers are pretty useless as far as the EP's overall pacing goes. Their brief arpeggios and sound effects make no effort to rectify this, either.

'Analoggins' (7:20) (Captain Voafose, Smojphace)
This is the only *Analord* track with a credit to someone other than James. The EP's Side 2 label tells us this was co-written with Captain Voafose – the alias of Jeremy Simmonds, who has also worked with Luke Vibert and Boymerang. If you thought this exterior influence might suggest it's a great track, you'd be wrong. It boils down to an uncomfortable miasma of acid burps, bleeps and messy vocal snippets that draws itself out for over seven tiring minutes.

2009 bonus tracks
'Bodmin 1' (4:36)
In its demo-like production, 'Bodmin 1' can seem as a spruced-up *GAK* track. To say that it adds much new to that overly-simple formula, would be an overstatement. It lays down a stock acid base and runs with it, stopping once or twice to add a new synth, and seems content with that minimum amount of work.

'Bodmin 2' (4:17)
Another forerunner of the languid *Cheetah* sound, 'Bodmin 2', is still underdeveloped. But at least it has some intriguing ideas, that could be pursued in a better form – for example, the 303 has a fine progression. This doesn't stop the rest from being more boilerplate acid techno, unfortunately.

'Bodmin 3' (5:26)
This begins with a processed bass line that sounds oddly like Depeche Mode's 'Nothing', and then continues down the average lane the two prior tracks travelled. This is the best of the three, dispatching some mildly captivating synth motifs, and sounds that are allowed to shine later on in spite of the generally-haphazard production.

Analord 07 (2005)

Release date: April 2005
Running time: 20:24; 24:09 (with 2009 bonus tracks); 28:56 (with Aphex Twin
website bonus track)

'Lisbon Acid' (8:29)

Rightfully regarded as one of the best *Analord* tracks (even one of the best
AFX songs overall), 'Lisbon Acid' is everything this series should aspire to be.
There's an overhanging sense of mystery and intrigue throughout, whether
that's courtesy of the post-punk thwack of the drums or the fug of floating
synths in the first half. Utilising its eight and a half minutes, the piece funnels
its initial eerie production into a concentrated dose of swirling acid glory,
with an infectious drive and purpose that herds the thick film of 303s and
sleek keyboards into a moment of sheer unbridled euphoria. Stunning.

'Pitcard' (6:18)

Whilst 'Pitcard' starts as a throwback to 'Green Calx', it soon develops into
a very Orbital-esque slice of acid techno – a comparison that comes as a
result of the trade-off between the slipping-and-sliding high-pitched synths
and the blanket of long-held notes. On the other hand, the acid furrows are
undoubtedly-Aphex. It's nowhere near as strong as 'Lisbon Acid', but another
energetic progressive-acid track shouldn't be taken for granted.

'AFX Acid 04' (5:37)

This is a bit of a destabilising finale considering the sudden tempo drop from
'Lisbon Acid', and the high-energy freneticism of 'Pitcard'. As such, 'AFX Acid
04' has the least surprises of the project, returning to the contented 303 funk
that appears all through the series. That it's the shortest track also indicates
that the more-detailed ideas were seized by its predecessors, and the track's
contents don't dispel that.

2009 bonus track
'Wabby Acid' (3:33)

Darting around like the fly in the song title, the synths here herald a step
back into frenzied acid. Unfortunately, even though the second half's bubbly
homage to Kraftwerk's 'Home Computer' changes things up a bit, the track
gets annoying very quickly, the 303's watery texture enhancing the grading
repetition of the ostinati.

Website bonus track:
'lisbon acid unedited original live mix' (8:32)

This alternative mix of the venerable 'Lisbon Acid' featured as a one-
off single on the Aphex Twin website. Sharing qualities with the other

purported parallel mixes of *Analord* tracks, this isn't a whole lot different from the EP variant, save for a few dynamic and mix changes. Thus, it's still an enrapturing experience, seemingly fully-formed from the start.

Analord 08 (2005)

Release date: May 2005
Running time: 20:33; 25:32 (with 2009 bonus track)

'PWSteal.Ldpinch.D' (3:44)

Continuing the tradition of spellbinding *Analord* openers, this is a delightful piece of acid techno, showing-off some of the best-sounding synths of any Aphex track. There's something comforting about the fuzzy production, which brings out the drum kit's crisp distortion and glaciers of bulky leads. Burning through hooks like nobody's business, the track reels you into its glorious sound world, and lets you linger in its vast beauty for a well-paced four minutes.

'Backdoor.Berbew.Q' (5:02)

Setting this EP apart from the rest in the sequence, James delves into minimal techno sounds, for the most part replacing the acid synths with older analogue keyboards, stapled onto a continuous, supple beat. Distinguished by the soundtrack cue stabs crammed in every few seconds, this track is commendable but relies too heavily on the less-than-subtle aspects in a subgenre where relative quiet is the key.

'W32.Deadcode.A' (6:34)

A much more accurate stab at creating a minimal techno beat, the drums are held back, content to reside in the sub-bass zone alongside the limber descending of the low-end keyboards. Ambient inflections are conveyed in the gaps in the sound spectrum, and lithe synth fills that bear the sole traces of the track's acidic influence. It's the longest track here, but the effortless grace and flawless production in flux make the time fly by.

'Backdoor.Spyboter.A' (5:13)

Somewhat of a fusion of the previous two tracks, the second 'Backdoor' invites the 303 back into the fray, as a techno riff rides stoically amongst the thin drum sound. The latter is measured and integrated deep within the structure so the flickers of synth can glide across a solid foundation. It comes close to being held back by the same repetition concerns as the first 'Backdoor', but has enough variety to retreat from this potential annoyance.

2009 bonus track
'Backdoor.Berbew.Q (Tollwedgechord Mix)' (4:59)

This is yet another alternative mix of a pre-existing track. Unfortunately, it's also a mix of the weakest track here, with (surprise) not much changed between the two versions. Therefore, it's an extremely disposable copy of an already-flawed track.

Analord 09 (2005)

Release date: June 2005
Running time: 16:34; 22:40 (with 2009 bonus track)

'PWSteal.Bancos.Q' (5:00)

As if to appease any listeners who thought the previous entry was light on the acid, this opener throttles you with its 303 attack right from the start. It's once again close to those earlier hardcore tracks, thereby struggling to emerge from a mind-numbing rut of unhinged background keyboards and an over-compressed mix making everything unnecessarily loud.

'Trojan.KillAV.E' (3:07)

Replicating the four-on-the-floor of the previous track, this has at least a few saving graces with the echoes of 'PWSteal.Ldpinch.D' in its mild bass tones and buried analogue leads. As for the rest, nothing deviates from the irritating model of the previous track, but thankfully it's less-drawn-out this time.

'W32.Aphex@mm' (3:57)

Again we have a near-carbon copy of the 'PWSteal.Bancos.Q' formula. I had to check if the last track hadn't repeated by accident, as the cocktail of 303 squawks, barely audible lead fills and thumping techno beat was indistinguishable from it. It goes without saying that – consequently – it made little impression on me.

'Backdoor.Netshadow' (4:49)

Generics abound once more. The homogenous influences come to the fore for the fourth time in a row, but with a noticeably-more-empty mix being taken up by a stock, crazed bass line. By this point, the machine-line regularity of below-mediocre pieces makes any intended dementia seem soulless, unfortunately.

2009 bonus track
'Liptons B Acid' (5:47)

At last, something that attempts to diverge from the mould! To be frank, 'Liptons B Acid' isn't an all-time great, but at this stage, any slight sonic changes are welcome. Re-routing the bulk of the track to the melodic side of things – what would seem to be standard fare on most of the other EPs in its mixture of constantly whirring detail – is a godsend after this gruelling project.

Analord 11 (2005)

Release date: June 2005
Running time: 19:26; 37:15 (with 2009 bonus tracks)

'W32.Mydoom.AU@mm' (8:48)

A world away from the rote forms of *Analord 09*, the first track on the final entry in the long series is a psychedelic trip into an electronic void. Growing from the unassuming seeds of a few synth drones and disjunct motifs, it eventually blooms into a murky odyssey full of keyboards dripping with chorus and ominous intervals. Making great use of the stereo environment to enhance the gaping space between the instruments, the track is a trepidatious journey into alien worlds; danger omnipresent in every sound chosen.

'VBS.Redlof.B' (4:38)

Rarely heard in the *Analord* series, sampled drums power the rubbery bass line and thrumming, buzzing synths for this fantastic reimagining of older post-punk forays into electronics. The throbbing chordal movements date back to OMD's 'The New Stone Age' and the bass motif of The Cure's 'A Forest'. Coming to a head with a busy drum section and atonal noise, this track is loose but pleasantly awkward: post-punk in microcosm.

'Backdoor.Ranky.S' (6:00)

The funereal arcade bleeps and bloops seem to be an audio representation of a computer's the dying breaths; the Pac-Man synths being actively entombed beneath the muffled production. Whines and howls flit about as the instrumentation struggles to keep itself going, with elongated drones marking the climax of these final moments – fitting since it's the last proper *Analord* track, and is a bleak send-off.

2009 bonus tracks

'Not Disturbing Mammoth 1 (Mono)' (2:05)

A perplexing snippet, made up of a fuzz bass riff and a wobbly bird-chirp synth that repeats for two minutes and leaves, no clearer than when it started.

'Not Disturbing Mammoth 2 (Mono)' (2:00)

In isolation, this sub-bass and drums track is worthless. But when played beside 'Mammoth 1', it makes a bit more sense, complementing that track's melodic side in a forgettable way.

'Love 7' (4:45)

Bonus track fodder in a nutshell, 'Love 7' is pleasing to the ear, but in the end, it is an anonymous piece. The vocal samples – pitched up and down and fed through a tremolo effect – are a cool touch, and are echoed by the gated synths in the backdrop. But it abides by the *Analord* rulebook too closely to warrant relistening.

'3 Notes Con' (4:54)

The innocence of the low-attack lead synth, contrasts with the snarling, gritty bass that surprisingly veers into electro-swing with a 6/8 drum rhythm. The sound choices are inspired, ranging from plucky low-end stabs to vaporous treble sections. But it offers nothing new after the beat starts, though it stands well above a lot of the other bonus material.

'VBS.Redlof.B (Bass Version)' (3:28)

The last *Analord* song overall is (What else could it be?) an alternate mix. Pushing the bass and stampeding percussion to the top of the track (alongside the noise elements flirted with in the original track), this version misses out on that variant's accomplished post-punk touches by relegating the melody to a two-note riff played on some irksome synths.

AFX / LFO (2005)
Alias: AFX

Personnel:
Richard D. James: Producer, performer (AFX tracks)
Release date: August 2005
Chart placings: Did not chart
Running time: 7:37 (AFX tracks)
Record label: Warp Records

A real curio in the Aphex catalogue is this split EP with Warp labelmates LFO. Each artist contributes two tracks to what was an item exclusive to Warp's subsidiary label Warpmart – meaning that only 2000 copies were pressed. The record was housed in a clear plastic sleeve. Since this is a book about Aphex Twin, I'll only include the two tracks he wrote and produced.

'46 Analord-Masplid' (4:41)

Slightly more complex than the following track, this track still plunders from the repetitive tropes of hardcore acid, with its creaking loop and synth-noise outbursts. At least the drums have a sense of drive, offering some rhythmic confusion towards the end.

'Naks 11 (Mono)' (2:56)

A basic acid piece, reminiscent of some of the *Analogue Bubblebath* material of the mid-1990s. A 303 loop repeats throughout, along with some slight drum programming and thin bass. It's really not worth seeking out.

Confederation Trough (2007)
Alias: The Tuss
Personnel:
Brian Tregaskin (Richard D. James): Producer, performer
Release date: April 2007
Chart placings: Did not chart
Running time: 15:31 (CD); 15:12 (Vinyl)
Record label: Rephlex Records
All music by Brian Tregaskin (Richard D. James)

This was the debut of James' then-newest pseudonym The Tuss. Closely
linked with *Rushup Edge* (the Tuss album released in June), both covers
have pictures of ram and are credited to the elusive Brian Tregaskin – a
name used to retain the project's secrecy, though there were still murmurs of
James' involvement. *The Guardian*'s May 2007 article 'Dancing in the Dark'
did some detective work on the matter, going as far as inquiring if Brian was
doing any interviews. But for the most part, all this wasn't as widely accepted
as it is now.

   The vinyl and CD versions differ in their closing tracks. 'GX1 Solo' brings
the curtain down on the CD, whereas 'Akunk' finishes the vinyl. The former
refers to the Yamaha GX-1 synthesizer, that was the first large polyphonic
keyboard the company produced. Sound-wise, the EP continues on the acid
techno and analogue synth pathway sketched out in the *Analord* series,
cementing this as James' default ongoing composition mode.

'Fredugolon 6' (5:34)
This is a drunken fever dream, helped by the dazed flanging of the drums
and synths, and the percussive struggle against the drooling keyboards. This
foreboding opening is softened by the microtonal thrum of the rich synth
pads and fruity bass, uncovering a few crystalline melodies in the process
before slipping into the inebriated instrumental selection once again.

'Alspacka' (4:53)
A taut tribute to the Detroit techno forefathers, 'Alspacka' is clipped synth
funk at its finest. The percussion *pops*, the bass *stabs* and the synth pads
glissade, all flanked by the robust arpeggiator to keep everything well within
the pocket. The last minute sees the three-dimensional piece come alive
again, as the tart low-end trickles through the fingers of the angelic chords
shining above.

'GX1 Solo' (5:01)
This is confusing immediately, as the time signature changes from 4/4
to a 3/4 swing once the now-familiar dollops of synth pad and 303 are
administered. Lacking control over its own structure, the song darts

sporadically between fizzing atonal effervescence and measured melodic interaction: making it a disjointed – though perfectly acceptable – closer.

'Akunk' (4:42)

A distorted trip-hop beat is guarded by vibrant portamento and a tough shell of bass manoeuvres: a rare sight this far into the Aphex discography. The most bizarre thing about this choice of backing is that the rest of the sounds unravel in less time-bound ways, falling into a fragmented state similar to 'GX1 Solo', but more consistently due to their closely interlocking state.

Album: Hangable Auto Bulb (Compilation) (2005)
Alias: AFX
Personnel:

Richard D. James: Producer, performer

Release date: October 2005

Chart placings: Did not chart

Running time: 34:18; 41:24 (2017 website reissue)

Record label: Warp Records

In 2005, Warp combined and repackaged the two 1995 *Hangable Auto Bulb* EPs to commemorate their tenth anniversary. Adorned with a new cover, this compilation had no new bonus material when it was released on CD, but in 2017 it was expanded on the Aphex Twin website with the two below unreleased tracks.

'get a baby' (2:27)
Utilising more samples from *Children Talking*, 'get a baby' is a sweet, delicately-proportioned drill-'n'-bass track. Instead of being on the attack, the percussion traipses around the plucked melody sparkles, scraping across the moody pads, laying out glistening chords underneath. It's more than worthy of a place on any of the EPs, and the melodic focus has the most in common with the stacks of hooks present on the next entry.

'choirDrilll' (4:12)
'choirDrilll' is abundantly percussive, running the gamut of James' rhythmic settings, to spiral into organised chaos. The gated melody that creeps in therefore becomes a weightless motif that brings the mournful choral aspect and the intently-propulsive duality of the title into focus. It's probably the closest the project gets to the nostalgic reveries of the *RDJ Album*, and that's a massive compliment.

Album: Rushup Edge (2007)
Alias: The Tuss

Personnel:
Karen Tregaskin (Richard D. James): Producer, performer
Release date: June 2007
Chart placings: Did not chart
Running time: 32:43 (Original); 55:59 (2017 website re-issue)
Record label: Rephlex Records
All music by Karen Tregaskin (Richard D. James)

The first and only album released under the Tuss moniker, *Rushup Edge* continues the sound of *Confederation Trough*, lengthening the tracks and adding even more compositional detail. The album is named after a ridge in the Peak District. *Rushup Edge* is credited to Karen Tregaskin: apparently the fictional Brian's sister. The vinyl and CD versions contained the same six tracks, though, interestingly, the former was split across three 7" 45-rpm discs with one track per side.

In 2017, a wealth of unreleased tracks appeared as album addendums on the Aphex Twin website. This digital reissue also altered all the titles by adding letters, or – as in the case of 'Death Fuck' – retitling them completely. Some of these had appeared that year on a self-released cassette nicknamed the *Mt. Fuji 2017 Cassette*, which was made especially for the Fuji Rock Festival.

'Synthacon 9' (6:22)
Somehow compressing dozens of moving parts into one six-minute track, 'Synthacon 9' is a progressive-synth masterclass; every bar containing something new. Enchanting bass oscillations collide with spectral synth outlines, while the drums encounter plateaus of vocoder and oceans of fluid sequencer programming as they wind through handclaps and tom-tom fills. On paper, it seems overwhelming, with little to hang onto amid the dense web of musical elements. But the execution dispels any of those concerns, as the production gives them all ample room to breathe and gloriously unfurl.

'Last Rushup 10' (6:36)
Just as heavily compartmentalised and concentrated as 'Synthacon 9', 'Last Rushup 10' begins opaquely, with a sinister, percolating, chromatic, vocoder-led groove that blooms into a magnificently-understated landscape of pads and in-the-pocket drum loops. The unison phrasing in the second half is unnervingly funky, whilst the drums again reach for drill-'n'-bass complexity. It's brilliantly crafted and winningly awe-inspiring, as usual.

'Shiz Ko E' (3:08)
Beginning with a loose elasticity that people forget *can* emanate from supposedly-stiff electronica, 'Shiz Ko E' is piecemeal compared to the other

tracks here. Still, it manages to include a reversed drum section, vocoder interjections, a blinding icy synth riff and a flexible bass motif.

'Rushup I Bank 12' (4:41)

The disjointed and somewhat demented opening synth musings are almost immediately contextualised by the rubbery comfort of the bass riff. It leads to a romantic piano solo, before scaling mountains of distorted acid synth to reach a heavy drum-'n'-bass section; not to mention the majestic chord movement throughout, and the stadium-sized production that caps off another sublime piece.

'Death Fuck' (Re-titled 'H949' on the 2017 reissue) (6:39)

The most crushing Aphex drum track since 'Quoth' on *Surfing on Sine Waves*, 'Death Fuck' revels in its exaggerated glory by just letting the rhythm section run wild over everything else. So unbridled is the percussion, the dainty piano runs and forbidding synth notes are barely able to contain the adjacent breakcore fury. It's a testament to James' that these tonal elements are prevented from being lost in the flood of atonality washing over it.

'Goodbye Rute' (5:22)

Perhaps inevitably, such a blazingly-fast album would need to end on a slower track to allow the listener to finally catch their breath. Bringing ambient touches absent from the rest of the EP, 'Goodbye Rute' is fine with wallowing in its measured array of synth ostinati for its duration. While those motifs aren't as attractive as some of the others on the project, the chosen tones are a perfectly relaxed finish.

Website bonus tracks
'goodbye jo (original live mixdown)' (4:05)

This sounds like a prototype for 'Goodbye Rute', containing a similar blend of rounded synth patches and unhurried drum loops. The production is excellent, with the upfront atmosphere of a live set distilled into crisp quality. If only the actual composition could match the track's overall sound.

'1st rushup m, +3' (2:17)

This is a fairly average acid techno track, at least when viewed through the lens of its basic elements. Thankfully, James embellishes it with luxurious synth pads that properly sustain the album's slightly threatening mood when mapping out dissonant intervals. It passes by in an instant, but is relatively engaging while it's here.

'computerband 2000 m, +3' (2:22)

Made on a – surprise! – Computerband 2000 synth, this goofy song sounds like Tom Waits circa *Rain Dogs* being fed through a chiptune filter. Under that primitive dressing, there's an almost-polka bass figure and minor chord changes that could've come straight from a 1980s Waits song. However, it's a little too slight to cement much of a place in the catalogue.

'oslo 2 +6.1' (2:52)

Another curious bonus, this is underpinned by a sampled hip-hop-esque drum loop, built on with a dub-inspired landscape filled with echoing synths and sound effects smothered in delay. But like the preceding number, it just doesn't have enough weight to have any long-lasting effect.

'(S770/SCI 3000, powertran) beautiful Japanese people' (4:57)

This is one of the two tracks included on the *Mt. Fuji 2017* tape and is the best Tuss bonus by far. It's certainly the softest of any of this side project's compositions, taking an off-kilter, spongy synth motif and slotting it into a psychedelic mix of chiming bells, phaser effects and moaning, languorous drones. This is all centred around a pentatonic progression, incorporating the Japanese subject matter straight into the fabric of the music itself. Frankly, it's disgraceful that it wasn't included on the album – it's *that* good.

'talkin2u mix2 +9' (3:08)

According to the addendum affixed to this on the Aphex Twin website, the track uses an old ETI vocoder bought off Steve Thomas. The second of the two *Mt. Fuji* tracks, the vocoder is featured prominently throughout, dodging the unhurried drum rhythm and whining Prophet notes. But ultimately, the slower tempo doesn't gel well with the album's more-frantic offerings.

'stride portugal' (3:33)

Picking up the tempo, 'stride portugal' is the antithesis of 'talkin2u...' – long, twisted branches of 303 punctuated by drill-'n'-bass percussion flair, wind through scattered synth sections. It follows the maxim of introducing copious new elements as it progresses, making it a more-than-solid closer for The Tuss' body of work.

Album: Caustic Window (released 2014; recorded 1992-94)
Alias: Caustic Window
Personnel:
Richard D. James: Producer, performer
Release date: June 2014
Chart placings: Did not chart
Running time: 68:27
Record label: Rephlex Records

You may be wondering what an album recorded in the early-1990s is doing here so late in the chronology. This eponymous Caustic Window album was left unreleased for years, and only a few test pressings exist. So, what makes this different from *Analogue Bubblebath 5:* another generally-unreleased project? Well, in 2014 – 20 years after it was recorded – one of only five test pressings was put up for sale on Discogs at the eye-watering price of $13,500.

Soon, a deal was struck with Rephlex and the online electronic music forum We Are The Music Makers, the price was brought down (to a slightly more manageable £5,000) and 500 users were given the chance to get a digital copy, meaning that – unlike the aforementioned *Analogue Bubblebath 5 –* there's a widespread, official digital version of the album. It was also agreed that the physical test pressing would be put up for sale on eBay after the forum auction finished. The donations fed into an online Kickstarter program that eventually raised over $47,000 for James and the charity Doctors Without Borders. To make things even stranger, the person who eventually purchased the test pressing was none other than Markus Pearson (also known as Notch): the creator of the video game *Minecraft*. The final selling price came to just under the amount raised on Kickstarter: a massive $46,300.

Inevitably, the album quickly made its way online, with high-quality versions existing on Soundcloud and YouTube for anyone to hear. Musically, the LP flicks between moments of IDM and ambient techno, with tracks in the acid house and techno vein, more in line with the other Caustic Window releases. Perhaps surprisingly, the critics received it very well, with publications like *Pitchfork* and *Consequence of Sound* praising it.

'Flutey' (8:20)
This lengthy, repetitive, minimal techno track revolves around a four-bar bass phrase and tender sprays of hi-hat and ticklish kick drum. Everything is downplayed. Each new loop – whether a melodic or rhythmic motif – is tightly woven into the instrumental. Constantly pressing forward, these eight minutes truly fly by: so hypnotic is the thicket of grooves.

'Stomper 101mod Detunekik' (7:26)
Already mining much harsher territory than the opener, this anticipates the scalding percussive attack of 'Ventolin' one year early, cranking up the

distortion and atonality. Still, shreds of ambient material find their way in, enhancing the contrast. But it dilutes its intended aural punch by stretching itself over seven minutes.

'Mumbly' (5:32)
Interweaving dialogue from the film *From the Terrace*, 'Mumbly' is an underrated IDM banger. Re-appropriating the 'Xtal' drum rhythm, James layers glistening analogue synths and an anticipatory, ascending motif. The sampled dialogue is, for the most part, well-integrated, and the whole track is able to balance atmosphere and rave-worthy catharsis.

'Popeye' (1:19)
An inessential interlude consisting of just a two-bar techno loop laden with distortion. But it disturbs the album's flow, and is therefore very out of place.

'Fingertrips' (4:17)
This is a throwback to late-1980s acid house and the cymbal-led tracks James was creating around that formative time. Things take a turn for the better, though, when the lovely ambient chord pads come swooping in, morphing into appropriately-trippy syncopated synth movements. It's a more-than-capable track to realign the course of the album.

'Revpok' (3:43)
Sort of a middle ground between the combative musical elements thus far, 'Revpok' weds a hardcore techno beat to the psychedelic swirl of the starry-eyed synths. The latter parts are the saving grace here, as – in its unrelentingly compressed form – the rhythm section carries over uncomfortable memories of the early, grading EPs.

'AFX Tribal Kik' (1:06)
This is more consequential than 'Popeye', by virtue of the techno beat's novel and vaguely tribal rhythms. That doesn't mean it's an integral part of the album. In fact, it's almost as disposable as 'Popeye', thanks to its dearth of development.

'Airflow' (5:06)
'Airflow' circles around a heavily-gated synth motif that ends up being one of James' most-poppy melodies; its appeal only strengthened by the woodwind timbre of the held keyboard notes reverberating alongside it. The beat is admittedly cumbersome, but the cavernous space around it counters any accusation of the track being leaden.

'Squidge in the Fridge' (4:09)
A straight house cut, 'Squidge in the Fridge' predicts the sound of the *Analord* series ten years early, with a strong emphasis on texture and

melody. The airy pads are anchored by the squishy 303, while the gently-percussive and syncopated piano plays off the negative space left by the drums. It's devilishly simple, yet so wonderfully effective.

'Fingry' (4:51)

Initially a disruptive techno number, 'Fingry' doesn't wait long before it transitions into a standard Aphex acid track. Church-like synth patches bleed into the rigid stretches of groggy bass and tambourine-inflected percussion loops. But there's a little too much of the latter, and not enough of the more-enticing former.

'Jazzphase' (3:24)

The jazz fusion of Herbie Hancock's *Head Hunters* seems to be the main influence on this untypical track. The combination of funky electric piano and deep bass, recalls 'Chameleon' from that watershed record. But in truth, the quality of this average cut is more in line with the similarly-fusion-indebted *Expert Knob Twiddlers*.

'101 Rainbows Ambient Mix' (8:52)

The single track that takes you completely off-guard and truly reminds you of the pure Aphex magic, is this one – a timeless piece that sounds like an electronic relic from a distant future, caked in a filter effect that sprinkles an indescribable aura over the rich sequencers and floating woodwind notes. Only minute changes occur as it progresses.

Like the works on *SAW Volume II*, we're given the opportunity to see the natural effect of time on the piece, as if we're only viewing it at one stage in its long musical life. Thus, we hear bursts of birdsong-like arpeggios, the decay of the main sequencer motif, and fragments of percussion invited into the spellbinding whole. It's masterful, and, honestly, one of a kind.

'Phlaps' (3:50)

Snapping the listener out of the '101 Rainbows' reverie, 'Phlaps' is a bleeping mess of wailing siren synths and masochistic drum loops. As a whole, it's closer to a harsh noise wall than anything else. This is confirmed with the addition of the later grinding synth sounds, making it even more intensely irritating.

'C**t' (4:16)

The album's last proper track is a blazing cacophony that's the type of hyper-tumultuous cut James would conclude one of his recent DJ sets with. The use of noise elements overall comes off more accomplished than 'Phlaps''s dabbling, and the title's confrontational swearing is echoed in the closing clangour of speeding gritty synths.

'Phone Pranks (Part 1 & 2)' (2:16)

Multiple recordings of James making prank phone calls: split into two parts. I'd be extremely shocked if anyone actively seeks this one out.

Album: Syro (2014)
Alias: Aphex Twin

Personnel:

Richard D. James: Producer, piano, synthesizer, keyboards, drums, percussion, vocoder, programming

Mandy Parnell: Mastering (2-13)

Beau Thomas: Mastering (1)

Release date: September 2014

Chart placings: UK: 8, US: 11

Running time: 64:31 (Original); 69:50 (Website)

Record label: Warp Records

When *Syro* was released, it had been 13 years since the last mainline Aphex Twin album. As we've seen, James hadn't been exactly dormant. Alongside the *Analord* series and various Tuss projects, he'd continued to DJ live as Aphex Twin, even previewing some songs that would feature on the upcoming LP.

The *Syro* tracks had been brewing for around five years, following the three-year-long construction of James' new studio, which was fraught with setbacks. In 2014, James told *Pitchfork* interviewer Philip Sherburne that his engineer was wiring patch bays together for 'about three months, every day', before realising that 'he was doing it all wrong and had to start again'. James confirmed that – perhaps as a result of the mistake – the tracks were made in six different studios. Thankfully, the eventually finished studio galvanised James to try different setups and instrumental combinations. In the *Pitchfork* interview, he stated that he would 'just get bored and swap things out' instead of having to 'keep the same bloody setup for more than five minutes'. Inevitably, the long timespan and range of recording areas resulted in a large arsenal of equipment being used across the album. The deluxe edition contains a 'disinfographic' detailing the 138 instruments and production units that were utilised on the album.

Perhaps unsurprisingly, the album's sound was governed by James' arsenal of electronics, effectively fusing the complex and progressive qualities of the longer tracks on *Drukqs* with the analogue sound of the *Analord* series. Also, James incorporated aspects from acid breaks (with the low-pass filtered sound of the 303)and skweee: a Sweden/Finland-based offshoot of electro that combines funk bass lines with chiptune-inspired leads: something James helped pioneer. Arguably, it's James' least-inventive album overall, but he reassured people that that was his intention, saying in the *Pitchfork* interview, 'There's nothing I need to explore more'.

When it came to teasing the album's existence – in line with previous rollouts – publicity stunts were the key. But instead of the Chris Cunningham collaborations providing the necessary shock to gain buzz, James started this viral marketing trail with a neon-green blimp bearing the Aphex Twin logo stylised inside the digits '2014', released over East London. Then, over in New York, several locations – including the prestigious Radio City Music Hall – were marked with Aphex Twin logo graffiti on the same day. All this culminated in the official Aphex Twin Twitter account two days later, posting a link to a website only visible by using the Dark Web software Tor – a link that led to an announcement showing the album title and tracklist.

The first Aphex Twin single in fifteen years – 'minipops 67 (source field mix) (120.2)' – was released ahead of the record on 4 September, which inspired predictions that the album would be a more-poppy offering. Production-wise, it's certainly lighter on the ears than *Drukqs* or *ICBYD*, but many tracks had few of the hook that would be required for it to constitute as pop. Nevertheless, the album gave James the best chart placing of his whole career – debuting at 8 in the UK, and 11 in the US: a major achievement for any musician. Sales increased when the album won a Grammy for Best Dance/Electronic album in 2015. To date, it's the last full-length Aphex Twin album. Like *Drukqs,* and maybe even more so than that album, it has sparked virtually another decade's worth of high-profile, seemingly relentless releases, which – whatever you think of *Syro* – must be credited to the album's catalytic effect.

'minipops 67 (source field mix) (120.2)' (4:47)

The so-called *comeback* single provided the first taste of *Syro*, and it couldn't have done a better job. Utilising a footwork-adjacent beat (at 120 bpm, as the number in brackets tells us) that stutters as readily as the rest of the music is robust, James layers a pungent array of synths that colour the mix – from depth-charge bass and uneasy plucky tones, to choir samples and interrupted acid squalls. What's more, he tosses out unique hooks and melodies like commodities – whether it's the burbling, phased vocal motif (his most-poppy use of the human voice since 'Windowlicker') or the rushes of piano that fill the lulls of the oscillating composition. All of it contributes to a resoundingly one-of-a-kind piece that functions simultaneously as a masterclass for all of James' new disciples in his years of so-called absence.

'XMAS_EVET10 (thanaton3 mix) (120)' (10:31)

We move from the tightly-constructed pop of 'minipops', to this spaced-out, progressive synth jam stretched over a considered and luscious ten minutes. Tart bass slaps of clear synth-funk origins, rest under an ambient bed made of samples of James' family, outdoor field recordings and sepulchral pads. He also demonstrates his continued mastery of catharsis, tension and release to pace the epic. Moments arise that are purely orgasmic for the ears, like the rising 303 at the halfway point or the tinkling synth bells that come in soon after. It's groovy, engaging and altogether extraordinary.

'produk 29 (101)' (5:03)

If 'XMAS_EVET10' hinted at synth-funk influences, 'produk 29' revels in them. The production is delectable here. The bass sound is absolutely massive, governing over the recesses of synthetic sparkles and vocal samples (which are speculated to be from the reality show *Made in Chelsea*, oddly enough). Any moments that seem like they tread water are mostly made up for by the swagger of the beat and the textural variety on offer. Tempo-wise, it continues the more relaxed mood of 'XMAS...', wonderfully.

'4 bit 9d api+e+6 (126.26)' (4:28)

Picking up the pace now, this is a pleasant slice of quintessential Aphex acid, characterised by the subtle bass movements and divine synth slides. He even incorporates nudges toward pop again: intentional or not. The slapback-echo synths wouldn't seem out of place on a mid-2010s pop song, whilst the electric piano patch is fantastically-1980s-sounding. Skating through movements deftly, it's a superb blend of nostalgia and modernisation.

'180db_ (130)' (3:11)

This track could most plausibly slot into one of the *Analord* or Tuss EPs ('Fredugolon 9' comes to mind) due to the thumping techno beat giving way to an itchy break, and the microtonal waves of synth melted atop. Admittedly, it has less technical and compositional surprises than the best of the former or the standard for the latter. In fact, due to its dearth of discernible change, it's the album's slightest track.

'CIRCLONT6A (syrobonkus mix) (141.98)' (6:00)

This is one of many tracks here titled after the Cirklon sequencer across this LP and *Cheetah*, and is an acidified throwback to the mind-boggling epics of *Drukqs*; even using the distorted vocal of 'Afx237 v.7' at the beginning. True to form, the track starts off manically before somewhat coalescing into a magnificent melting pot of 303, skweee leads and fervent low-end working to create a sombre motif. The later redeployment of the head-scratching tremolo effect incorporates the studio as an active instrumental part, just as 'Mt. St Michel...' had 13 years prior. All things considered, it's a heady blend of things that makes even James' most complicated aspects so addictive and appealing.

'fz pseudotimestretch+e+3 (138.85)' (0:58)

Along with '180 db_', this is the closest thing to a dud on the album. It's a minute-long snippet of a decaying synth patch, garnished with some stray vocal manipulation on the front end. It's very much inessential.

'CIRCLONT14 (shrymoming mix) (152.97)' (7:21)

The ominous peal of analogue synthesizers heralds another lengthy excursion into an acidic bath of psychedelic electronica, where James pulls out his store of effects to maximise the disorientation radiated by the watery keys and oddly accented drum parts. Carrying on the lineage of previous similar tracks, it balances full-blooded IDM with quieter passages of tranquil decay, yet there aren't as many instantly-recognisable melodies stuffed among the peripheral electronics. Therefore, some parts are less cohesive and even a little forced when stacked against the effortless prior triumphs in this vein.

'syro u473t8+e (piezoluminescence mix) (141.98)' (6:32)
Bursting out of the gate with a stylish unison funk riff, the pseudo-title-track meshes exquisite Kraftwerkian keyboard manoeuvres and bleating arpeggios, to create a unique and stately but loose vibe. It seems James took whatever hooks he planned for 'CIRCLONT14' and implanted them here, since the variety of alternately-silken and serrated patches spit out one immense chord progression after the other. Of particular note is the forlorn sequence replayed after the halfway point, characterised by a downbeat murk of pads surrounded by an anxious party of spiralling licks and colourful percussive displays.

'PAPAT4 (pineal mix) (155)' (4:18)
In some ways, a sister piece to 'produk 29' (with an extra helping of drum-'n'-bass), 'PAPAT4' is brash and vibrant, anchored by the kind of peppy motif you'd find in an electroclash track. Familiar amen-break movements ensue as the keyboards remain in a tangle of bassy electrofunk. The sound choices *wow*, as usual, but you can't help but feel this track is unnecessary in the already lengthy tracklist, and that it could've easily been cut to improve the flow of the record's latter half.

's950tx16wasr10 (earth portal mix) (163.97)' (6:01)
One of the tracks previewed in embryonic form during live DJ sets in the years prior to the album's release, this track picks up the vintage drum-'n'-bass thread of 'PAPAT4'. But things don't remain standard for long, as you should expect by now. The recognisable drum loop soon becomes submerged in an ocean of gating effects and those evocative synth pads hear on earlier tracks. Close to the four-minute mark, room-shaking bass *wubs* and shimmering, bell-like keys, tear through the Byzantine walls of acid synth – the release feeling like a worthy energetic climax point for the LP.

'aisatsana (102)' (5:21)
A complete left turn from every other track before it, 'aisatsana' (James' wife's name spelt backwards) is a gentle piano piece. Field recordings at the periphery, highlight the frail phrases played on the Disklavier. Like the chamber jazz recordings of Talk Talk's Mark Hollis, silence and nature's *own* music play as big a role in the piece's emotional resonance as the melancholy chords being mapped out around them. This was no more apparent than

when James previewed this track at a 2012 Barbican performance, where the trusty Disklavier was swung like a pendulum across the hall to create a natural Doppler effect on the audience. The willingness to play so few notes, underlines James' continued growth as a composer. The entire performance and its surrounding elements, amount to one of James' greatest compositions.

Website bonus track

'end E2' (5:19)

According to the Aphex Twin website, this track was left off *Syro* for 'technical and personal reasons'. It's a real shame, as it's easily equal to the album's best tracks. Spongy synth textures paint a gorgeous three-note melody that's captivating in its redolent simplicity. Similarly, the drum tracks form an elaborate yet not overbearing lattice, bringing back the tones from 'Sloth' on *Analogue Bubblebath 4*. Coupled with the sighing vocals, it makes for an understated and remarkable finish.

The EPs, Part 8: 2015-2019

Computer Controlled Acoustic Instruments pt2 (2015)

Alias: Aphex Twin

Personnel:

Richard D. James: Producer, keyboards, percussion, programming

Release date: January 2015

Chart placings: UK: 36

Running time: 27:56 (Original); 40:30 (Website)

Record label: Warp Records

People who may have been worried about another long hiatus from James after *Syro*'s seemingly-constant media attention, had their fears put to rest with the release of this EP in January 2015. Described as a follow-up to *Drukqs* – the elusive 'pt1' preceding this – the project lives up to its title by consisting solely of midi-controlled electroacoustic experiments, widening the range of instruments used to include drums and other assorted percussion.

It proved to be a polarising project. *The Guardian* called some of the 'faster' pieces 'sometimes unlistenably irritating'. On the other hand, *Pitchfork* – the most positive reviewer of the EP – claimed that James 'comes in and executes perfectly'. The EP was somehow quite successful on the charts – even breaking the UK top 40 – despite its extremely experimental nature. That experimentation is what makes it one of the most individual releases in the Aphex Twin catalogue, for better or worse.

'diskhat ALL prepared1mixed 13' (5:22)

Setting out the EP's general sound, this begins ominously before lurching into a hip-hop beat accented by prepared-piano stabs and echoing mallet percussion. There's a definite air of uncertainty and uncanniness wafting through the instrumental interplay, despite the tight grooves. Nevertheless, this is the EP's most developed and constantly interesting ensemble piece.

'snar2' (0:20)

A 20-second, digitally-controlled snare drum solo with added dog bark.

'diskhat 1' (2:26)

Memorably used in the TV series *Better Call Saul*, 'diskhat 1' has one of the EP's best motifs, combining a dissonant bass piano with the tuned ringing of metallic percussion. Some of the atmospheric effects nudge it more into dub territory, but it's too deliberately awkward to pass as any kind of reggae.

piano un1 arpej' (0:50)

This barely-minute-long piano piece has clear echoes of 'Father' from *Drukqs*. Though this snippet doesn't have much meat on its bones besides a whirlwind of piano runs and a few lovely, stray, chords, it still evokes more than do the EP's most-clearly-programmed examples.

'DISKPREPT4' (1:53)

Utilising a range of percussive timbres feeding through each other like vines, 'DISKPREPT4' is built on a confounding blend of polyrhythms, adding semiquaver piano ostinati and syncopated upright bass. It's fine, but inessential: even in the EP's context.

'hat 2b 2012b' (1:25)

Working with a traditional drum kit, James plots out another solid hip hop groove across the cuckoo-clock chime of the ride cymbal and brushed snare, and is content to let it sit with the listener well past its novelty running out.

'disk aud1_12' (0:09)

Nine seconds of frantic piano and percussion runs.

'0035 1-Audio' (0:27)

Yet another drumkit-based hip-hop groove that at least cuts itself short so as not to become too stale.

'disk prep calrec2 barn dance (slo)' (4:22)

Finally, a longer track after the run of short preceding numbers. Confusingly titled 'barn dance', it wallows in a rhythmic fog that could pass for an improvisational segment of an ECM jazz track. Like many tracks here, it falters with the proportion of ideas and interest to length – the latter continuing to outweigh the former.

'DISKPREPT1' (3:30)

This combines descending hip-hop bass figures and chattering prepared piano over the course of multiple compositional switch-ups that – while not being that cohesive – at the very least justify a slightly longer runtime: keeping the listener on their toes for once.

'diskhat2' (0:38)

Finally fusing the solo drum kit and prepared-piano elements, 'diskhat2' possesses a fine syncopated groove that introduces itself and swiftly exits before any development is allowed to occur.

'piano un10 it happened' (1:48)

Without a doubt, the best track here, this ranks among the best Aphex piano pieces alongside the cream of *Drukqs* and 'aisatsana'. Using contrary motion between the semibreve-based low-end and the arpeggios in the treble (harkening back to 'Avril 14th'), James outlines a forlorn and secluded motif

119

that moves through a traditional structure without a hint of irony. As the notes briefly hang in the air, we can finally – 12 songs in! – hear the potential for heart amid the stiff, digitally-controlled landscape.

'hat5c 0001 rec-4' (4:46)
Recycling constituent parts from previous tracks (the swinging beat, the Tom Waits-esque grumpy bass phrases), this track piles on disconcerting drones, solitary piano notes and heavily-reverberated strings. The strict beat seems to weigh down the untethered atmospherics, summarising the dichotomous nature of the EP as a whole.

Website bonus tracks
'diskhat ALL prepared1mixed (snr2mix)diskhat ALL prepared1bmixed (snr2mix), e, ru, +4' (5:22)
This is a different version of 'diskhat ALL prepared1mixed 13' (with an even longer title!) that seems to be unmastered. The sounds are a lot drier than their EP counterparts, and overall, the mix isn't as full as that version. Thus, it's difficult to prefer this over the one we actually got.

'diskhat ALL (snr2mix) (fast), e, +3' (4:52)
A second re-working of 'diskhat ALL...', this time sped up a little. But underneath, it's basically the same as the previous two versions. Though it's an interesting gimmick, the original's slower crawl is far preferable to this energised take.

'DISKLVPRPT1 Equinox barn dance(fast)' (2:20)
This is a sped-up variant of 'barn dance'. Like the previous version of 'diskhat', it loses a lot of the atmosphere that more often than not, prevents these tracks from tumbling into completely thin compositions. The spaces between the instruments mostly inject life into these pieces: an element forgone here.

MARCHROMT30A edit 2b 96 (2015)
Alias: Aphex Twin
Personnel:
Richard D. James: Producer, performer
Release date: April 2015
Chart placings: Did not chart
Running time: 18:04
Record label: Warp Records

An addendum to *Syro*, the title track was originally a bonus track on that album's Japanese version. In April 2015, it was pressed onto a white-label

12" with two exclusive B-sides for worldwide release: a new mix of 'XMAS_
EVET10' and a fast variant of the title track.

'MARCHROMT30A edit 2b 96' (7:19)

Along with 'end E2', this would've been another worthy addition to *Syro*.
Containing a punchy synth riff that sounds tailor-made for stadiums, the track
extrapolates this source of sweet, glistening melody, scattering it throughout its
sheets of shuffling drums and up-front bass slides. Comparisons to *SAW 85-92*
aren't unjustified, and while it doesn't quite hit the highs of that album, the epic
sound – tempered by lapping waves of ambience – is glorious to behold.

'XMAS_EVET1 N' (5:09)

A remix of 'XMAS_EVET10' that unfolds in half the time the languorous
original did. A casualty of this enforced brevity is that the LP version's airy
and spacious aura is tossed away. On the whole, the mix is emptier and drier.
Granted, the elements at the heart of the piece are still present: nullifying
some of the cut's inherent redundancy.

'MARCHROMT38 fast' (5:36)

For once, a sped-up mix that doesn't completely lose the power of the
original. In fact, 'MARCHROMT' works almost as well in this form. It
transitions from a protracted melodic exercise to an elastic *Analord*-esque
surge of billowing pads and full-bodied drum activity, managing to bisect the
original into two distinct yet closely related siblings.

Orphaned Deejay Selek 2006-08 (2015)
Alias: AFX

Personnel:
Richard D. James: Producer, performer
Beau Thomas: Mixing engineer
Release date: August 2015
Chart placings: UK: 34
Running time: 26:51 (Original); 45:49 (Website)
Record label: Warp Records

Mopping up some unreleased tracks that had lain dormant since their
inceptions between 2006 and 2008, *Orphaned Deejay Selek* marks the
reappearance of the AFX pseudonym last seen on the final *Analord* EP, ten
years prior. Remaining close in style to the sound palette of those projects –
but with a greater emphasis on percussion and rhythm – some of the tracks
are probably the closest James has come to out-and-out techno: at least since
'Quoth' from *Surfing on Sine Waves*.

Strangely – like the same year's *Computer Controlled Acoustic Instruments
pt2* EP – *ODS* (as it will be referred to henceforth) managed to get to 34

in UK, cementing James' revitalised public popularity. In 2017, the EP was enhanced on the Aphex Twin website by four bonus tracks which were released in physical form in 2019 as the *Manchester 20.09.2019* EP. This was originally sold exclusively at James' Manchester Warehouse Project show on that date, before a limited quantity was put up for sale during the show's livestream in December 2019.

'serge fenix Rendered 2' (3:16)

This is the EP's nearest approximation of the *Analord* sound, reusing the Fenix synth to lay down some gargantuan pads below the quaking drum machine and frantic arpeggiator. Flitting from one hectic motif to the next, the effect is drunken and uneven, prioritising confusion over the stability promised by the lush plains of synth at the start.

'dmx acid test' (1:17)

Running with the tempo of 'serge fenix...', 'dmx acid test' is a very slight acid composition, not daring to vary from its unremarkable raspy 303 riff, and spitting drum programming for its brief duration.

'oberheim blacet1b' (3:25)

Atonality continues to ensue on this next part of the pseudo-suite of the EP's first half. Although, mercifully, James permits some additional textures to colour the stale 303 looping. The Fenix proves its worth again, smoothing out the edges with its glacial glissade as a cymbal-based drum rhythm momentarily locates an intriguing groove.

'bonus EMT beats' (4:45)

This is James' version of a drum solo in an electronic context. Shuddering low-end takes precedence as he acts as a benevolent DJ – emphasising the reference to the beats tucked away on hip-hop 12"s – and tweaks the external effects, calling attention to certain parts of the unrelenting, hyper-detailed percussive mesh. This allows a potentially self-indulgent mess to become a more well-paced, sometimes enrapturing experience.

'simple slamming B 2' (3:51)

This is a near-unadulterated techno track until the familiar scrapes and skitters of the drill-'n'-bass snares and hi-hats, enter. The main melody is the sort of dissonant keyboard laser beam that can be found all over the 2017 *Field Day* EP. However, the clean production enables the less-distinguishable parts to take on a greater scale when placed together.

'midi pipe1c sds3time cube/klonedrm' (2:26)

Lying outside of the EP's typical sound palette, this track momentarily delivers us into a crude combination of the uncanny instrumentation of *Computer*

Controlled Acoustic Instruments and the droning slabs of sound from *SAW Volume II*, played on a custom midi pipe organ. Unfortunately, it has more in common with the former, feeling curiously empty rather than all-enveloping.

'NEOTEKT72' (6:09)

The track on the main EP to predicts James' musical direction for the next decade, 'NEOTEKT72' fashions a track out of the expansive – or at least longer – structures of *Syro*. Proving that the ideas in attendance on that LP weren't yet fully formed, the track lacks the catharsis that comes with the combination of melodic light-and-shade that the later songs typically possess. It goes on for six minutes but has very little to warrant its extension, save perhaps for the integration of the tuned percussion.

'r8m neotek beat' (1:42)

This weak closer is only moderately more developed than 'dmx acid test', and comes off like a song from *GAK*. It holds all the feeble qualities of those pieces, the mix being underfed with half-hearted percussion that's forgettable even while it's playing.

Website bonus tracks
'midi pipe2c edit +3' (4:09)

This sophomore outing for the midi pipe organ takes us back to the early-1990s through the fat bass tones and chopped-up, synth-scaling melodies. The real interest stems from James' cutting and editing, forming abnormal drum sounds from the random gating effects that slice through the robust groove.

'rozzboxv2mam+4' (4:35)

Made on the Rozzbox synth, this is more 1990s nostalgia, plunging into acid house with adroitness. The softly percolating 303 is a world away from the gritted-teeth growl the rest of the EP forces on it. In fact, all the keyboard timbres are generally more delicately thought out, finally making proper use of the continuously-clear production.

'pretend analog extmix 2b,e2,ru' (5:25)

'Recorded in the bank in 2004' – according to the Aphex Twin website – this is another acid-house throwback, with plenty of James charm audible throughout. The 303s are again phenomenal, skating between peaceful oscillations and foundational rhythms. Meanwhile, the pads hit the analogue sweet spot found on many an *Analord* track. Surfing into a swirl of creamy keys, this should've been a shoo-in for the EP.

'umil 25-01' (4:48)

Emerging from a mire of sound effects, a tart synth organ slaps against the stop/start rhythm throughout. Alongside this trebly pairing, the moody cries of washed-out keys, tickle the side of the mix. Clearly, the percussion is meant to be the focus, rotating through the quirky slivers of a drum-'n'-bass loop for the listener to heed in awe.

Cheetah (2016)
Alias: Aphex Twin
Personnel:
Richard D. James: Producer, performer
Beau Thomas: Mastering
Release date: July 2016
Chart placings: UK: 14, US: 140
Running time: 33:49 (Original); 36:26 (Website)
Record label: Warp Records

The next mainline Aphex Twin project is a curious one, bringing the analogue synth worship of the *Analord* series and *Syro* to new heights. The EP is even named after – and musically focused on – the British electronics company Cheetah Marketing and their notoriously difficult-to-program synth, the Cheetah MS800. Accordingly, the first taste we received of the project was at a designated booth at the NAMM (National Association of Music Merchants) show. True to James' sense of humour, the MS800 was displayed – alongside its manual – at a convention specialising in the newest developments in music technology.

In early June, many record stores received flyers depicting the EP's retro cover, which was a deliberate homage to 1970s advertising. It presented itself as a write-up of the MS800's features, making clear the nostalgic bent of the project's sound. On June 9, the EP was officially announced, and a few weeks later, on 21 June, the first single – 'CIRKLON3 (Колхозная mix)' – was released.

This single was mainly important for the fact that it had the first widely-released Aphex Twin music video since 'Windowlicker'. Instead of working with Chris Cunningham again, James had chosen Ryan Wyer, who was only 12 when commissioned to direct the video. James discovered Wyer's YouTube channel epic1:40d gaming, probably due to Wyer's creation of Aphex Twin review videos.

The video for 'CIRKLON3' has an appropriately childlike imagination, filmed in low, solarised quality. It mainly consists of Wyer and his friends dancing around in Aphex Twin masks, at variable speeds – retaining some of the disturbing qualities of the older Cunningham promos. The conflation of James' face and children, immediately recalls 'Come to Daddy'. It's genuinely great, and James' already-present influence on Wyer shows the range of individuals James has managed to appeal to over his career, thanks to his unique straddling of the musical and visual.

'CHEETAH2 (LD spectrum)' (5:53)

'CHEETAH2' sets out EP's general sound – dreamy, luminous electronic vistas mired in flanger and gooey textures. It's one of his smoothest tracks ever, which is both a compliment and a complaint. The production is indeed immaculate, and the warm blankets of synth are a feast for the ears. But there's no edge to it, and barely anything to distinguish it as James' work. Being so relaxed, it prevents itself from travelling outside its comfort zone to anything more worthwhile than nostalgic novelty.

'CHEETAHT7b' (6:43)

Stuck in the same rigid kick-drum-captained rut, 'CHEETAHT7b' takes even longer to emerge from the swampy phasing of bass licks and faded analogue keys. James leaves this basic mixture to wallow, adding tentative flickers of plucky chiptune synths as a means of development. Nonetheless, it's even more bereft of interest than the prior track, despite its pleasing timbres.

'CHEETA1b ms800' (0:27)

A 30-second jingle for the Cheetah, that swiftly builds from a tuning sequence to a kitschy payoff.

'CHEETA2 ms800' (0:37)

Waves of bit-crushed analogue chords make up this second interlude, fading in and out like tidal movements. It's as superfluous as its predecessor.

'CIRKLON3 (Колхозная mix)' (8:13)

The first of two more-accomplished tracks, 'CIRKLON3' serves up a glitchy, arcade-game soundtrack that returns somewhat to more-identifiably-Aphex musical qualities. The drums are altogether busier, and the bass darts along through stringy acid formations and more-weighty subs. Plus, there are reminders of the intricacy of older tracks in the sloping dynamics and outbursts of colourful funk synths. When viewed collectively, it's transparent that this is the meatiest cut here.

'CIRKLON 1' (7:17)

The drums are at their most fragmented on this track – a good chance of pace from the assembly-line regularity of the 'CHEETAH' tracks. Actually, the rhythm section has a more prominent role here, the crunchy bass tones engaging in some syncopated interplay with the feather-light lead synths. The latter go to great lengths to map out the EP's most-enthralling aspects, the closing panning motif being especially striking.

'2X202-ST5' (4:39)

Left off the vinyl issues, this perfunctory funky closer possesses a catchy spiralling bass line, cleverly mirrored by the other synths and not much else. Granted, it does gain a lot of mileage from that quality, but it's unsatisfactory as a final track. It's a cool idea that needed more time to be properly built on.

Website bonus track
'CIRKLON3(concentrate edit)' (2:37)
This extremely edited version of 'CIRKLON3', shaves off three-quarters of it, giving us the abbreviated highlights of the album's star track. Emphasising the most melodic parts, it would've made a good radio version to gain the single a wider audience.

Houston, TX 12.17.16 (Day for Night) (2016)
Alias: AFX
Personnel:
Richard D. James: Producer, performer
Beau Thomas: Mastering
Release date: December 2016
Chart placings: Did not chart
Running time: 20:46
Record label: Warp Records

This rare 12" release was almost exclusively sold at the 2016 Day for Night festival ahead of James' performance on 17 December. It set a precedent for future Aphex Twin concerts, with high-profile gigs like the ones at Field Day or the Printworks also gaining their own blank EP with either rare or previously-unreleased tracks included.

   Only 500 copies of this EP were pressed, but it was released onto the Aphex Twin website in 2019, simultaneously revealing the names of the previously-untitled tracks.

'no stillson 6 cirk' (10:48)
This makes a return to hardcore techno, and is an exercise in sustained tension. Populated by a fiery drone surrounded by pummelling beats, it acts as the ultimate EDM antithesis, refusing to move beyond its nervy buildup for 11 minutes. It's not the sort of thing that bears repeated listening, but it would work better (as other pieces have in the past) in a live context.

'no stillson 6 cirk mix2' (9:58)
Broadly identical to the first mix, the B-side take of 'no stillson' embellishes the shuffling percussive groundwork with extra helpings of buzzing synth, and threatens more often to explode into a moment of catharsis. Purely for the dedication to refuse this kind of aimless teasing, the A-side mix is better, but neither are favourites of mine.

London 03.06.17 (Field Day) (2017)
Alias: AFX

Personnel:
Richard D. James: Producer, performer
Release date: June 2017
Chart placings: Did not chart
Running time: 32:40 (Original); 72:05 (Website)
Record label: Warp Records

Continuing the example of *Houston TX*, *London 03.06.17* (also known as the *Field Day* EP) was sold in limited quantities at James' Field Day gig – one of his absolute finest DJ performances, which you can find the official stream of on YouTube. A number of tracks from this EP were played during his set, including some of the bonus tracks (which, cumulatively, are lengthy enough to be a project of their own), which were tacked onto the project on the Aphex Twin website a month later. A second update in 2019 added four further tracks to the end. Copies now reach almost £400 on Discogs, since the small run sold out swiftly after it was announced on the day of the concert.

'42DIMENSIT3 e3' (4:40)
Clusters of detuned synths open this track, shrouded in a fog of Mellotron and tunnelling arpeggios. Familiar beats are hit upon, as analogue synths slide around the clacking drum part. This sort of composition had become standard for James, so it didn't offer many new surprises. Nevertheless, it sets up the somewhat-threatening vibe strung throughout the EP.

'MT1T1 bedroom microtune' (3:47)
A potentially harmless cheap piano riff is manipulated and contorted – a theme that runs through the EP; the resolute kick drum thumping behind being the only constant. It amounts to an abstract acid techno track, as low bass grumbles and whirring synths butt in to increase the headache-inducing timbres.

'T18A pole1' (3:44)
More of the same sharp, brittle aesthetics remain embedded in this track. The anonymous beat gives no indication of the near-atonal synth patches that dart through a series of clanging, dissonant motifs. The investment in experimental tones is commendable, but the execution seems too confused and disorganized to gel as it needs to.

'T03 delta t' (4:01) start here
The first of this EP's tracks to be played at the Field Day show, 'T03...' is a smorgasbord of percussion. Industrial synth grinds, rub against the shaking drum programming, placing the track in an irregular time signature of 12/8.

Its rhythmic collage would be a great springboard for further embellishment, but James regrettably chose to leave it relatively untampered with, rendering it too bare for its own good.

'em2500 M253X' (1:50)
A diversion from the first four tracks, this strips the previously cluttered instrumental palette down to a warm synth patch and distant birdsong to increase the homely feeling the gently pulsating melody ekes out. Not dissimilar in tone and motivic development to Kraftwerk's 'Tanzmusik', it stands out by virtue of its charming melody and *verité* delivery opposing how busy the rest of the pieces are.

'T23 441' (2:51)
Another track played during the Field Day live set, this picks up where 'T03...' left off, shaping a constantly-shifting tempo that complements the out-of-control drum part. Everything is on the attack – the bass snarls as the trebly keys launch a terrifying riff operating on its own terms, offering enough substance to really thrill and surprise.

'42DIMENSIT10' (3:06)
Also played at the show, '42DIMENSIT10' feels like an expansion on the glitchy, lo-fi-recorded sections of 'Windowlicker'; having the same compressed tone. It's an unneeded extension, sadly. The production masks the shape-shifting synth cries so much that any subtlety is lost. The original source material worked only in the wider song's chameleonic context.

'T20A ede 441' (2:37)
A blazing synth drone ties down the murky cocktail of pads that drift in to fill the spaces left by the itchy percussion track. Murmured bubbles of melody rise out of this mixture, while the drums attempt to differentiate themselves with the placement of a few choice fills. It's one of the EP's more-cohesive and, therefore, likeable pieces.

'MT1T2 olpedroom' (1:57)
Detouring in the vein of 'em2500...', 'MT1T2' builds on that track's fragile melody with piercing keyboard squeals and altogether-unnecessary and bullying synth interjections. The techno beat also works against the insular motif, wasting a potentially appealing track with misguided additions.

'T47 smodge' (1:41)
If the title is meant to recall to the *Smojphace* EP, then the track only strengthens those ties, verging close to harsh noise in its heavily-delayed repurposing of the 'T03...' drum sounds. Even more than that EP's noise flirtations, it just feels clumsy as if it were an afterthought.

'sk8 littletune HS-PC202' (2:26)

Bit-crushed vocal samples echo into oblivion at the beginning of the original EP's closing track, with James utilising the snippet to create a disjointed and even-more-fragmented semi-motif. It goes to lengths to cement the EP's general success as a whole: a compelling concept somewhat nullified by its execution.

Website bonus tracks
'T13 Quadraverbia N+3' (3:14)

Some of the jittery *RDJ Album*-era programming virtuosity returns here, as the barely-there refrain is chopped-up to varying degrees of glitch. Thankfully, this reminder is present throughout. The rest of the track – aside from the 'T16.5...' tease – lacks melodic and timbral substance.

'T16.5 MADMA with nastya+5.2' (4:56)

This is a latter-day highlight, dropped into James' 2019 Printworks set to stunning effect. The track eschews the mostly-abstract bulk of this EP, and cranks out a *SAW 85-92*-type ambient techno banger that takes full advantage of the spacious production. The series of plucky, staccato riffs – from the chiptune fluctuations to the darker bass shifts that occur halfway through – have the same colourful and vibrant nature as the best of *Syro*, making it even more unbelievable that it was left as a web-exclusive bonus.

'T17 Phase out +3' (4:24)

A comedown after the ecstatic highs offered by 'T16.5...', 'T17...' delves back into the comfort of metallic emaciation. It's taken a step further by James obscuring most of the intricacies in the ricocheting synth notes and shrill, dissonant ostinati, leaving a scrawny drum part to carry itself for four minutes.

'T63 neotek 2h949 +3 (bonus beats)' (1:32)

This has a lot in common with the percussion-heavy tracks of *Orphaned Deejay Selek* – right down to the lean structure, grating loops and complete dearth of replay value.

'T08 dx1+5' (6:41)

Tangled webs of rhythm rebound off the walls over the course of this excursion. It's a kaleidoscope of chiming church bells, laser-focused tom rolls, stretched-out snare flams and mellifluous cymbal work. James lets the twisting percussive progression speak for itself, reminding us that he can be especially fleet-fingered and engaging with rhythm alone.

'T69T07 stasspa+3' (5:16)

This is a pretty normal acid jam, all things considered, with the presence of rich analogue synths and flexible 303 with a topping of a jerky drum pattern.

At this stage, it's perfectly listenable but has little of the subtle innovations of *Syro* or *Collapse*, of which its sound is closest to.

'T05 tx16w marion Mt***,e (sketches)' (4:04)

The tremolo percussion sound from 'T03...' comes back to haunt this track, though its placement is much more firm this time around. Wobbly synth tones circle around it, but it's crying out for something else to elevate these standard Aphex choices.

'T46 se70 rinseout2 (sketches)' (2:19)

Breaking the tame run of tracks before this, 'T46...' just feels like James goofing off, manipulating and detuning some ear-splitting synths for the hell of it. Besides shock value, there's nothing to warm to here.

'ZT01 (sketch1)' (3:10)

Throbbing sub-bass injections usher in ghostly double-tracked synths and droning pads. But the latter's titanic majesty would've been better without the insistent low-end and skirting drum patterns.

'TXT1+4 ds8 flngchrods(sketch0.1b)' (3:47)

Introducing parts from the drum-'n'-bass idiom, the unpronounceable closer is sadly a feeble one. The farting synths in the left channel are needlessly cumbersome when the rest of the mix is relatively light – a juxtaposition worsened by the fact that the jolly ascending chord progressions are themselves outcasts from the more-creepy climate the remaining tracks inhabit.

Korg Trax+Tunings for Falling Asleep (2017)
Alias: AFX

Personnel:
Richard D. James: Producer, performer
Release date: July 2017
Chart placings: Did not chart
Running time: 23:31
Record label: Korg

A collaboration between James and Tatsuya Takahashi – a former engineer for the electronics company Korg – this EP was made as a demo for the new Korg Monologue that the pair worked on together. James contributed his knowledge and passion for micro-tuning to create exclusive patches and tunings as synth presets.

The first two tracks here were made using only Korg gear. According to James, this included the Monologue, Minilogue and Volca Keys for the melodic parts, while the Volca Beats and MS-20 were used for the drums. He also sampled his son's voice using the Volca sampler. The remaining pieces are all demonstrations of the different tuning sequences James produced for use on the keyboard. I will not be covering these, as there are so many of them that are too broadly similar to each other to warrant separate discussion.

'Korg Funk 5' (3:27)

First released on a separate AFX/Korg collaborative EP, this is way better than any product demo deserves to be. As funky as its namesake suggests, it follows in the footsteps of its predecessor 'Fenix Funk 5', with an even tighter focus on groove, compounded by the bulky synth timbres and phased drum programming. Even the addition of the moody keyboard pads only serves to reinforce the delectable bass and lead interplay. If this and 'Korg Funk 5' were paired as a single, they would undoubtedly stand near the top of James' side outputs.

'Korg 1b' (3:00)

This is a similarly-strong slice of unashamedly-danceable acid house, complete with some of James' exclusive tunings dropping in as the arpeggiated backbone. Acrid spurts of 303, fly out from nowhere – indicating that this would've been a fantastic addition to the *Analord* series – before reversed synth grinds crash in to upset the delicate balance between the shuffling drum fills and rich keyboard patches.

Orphans (2017)
Alias: AFX

Personnel:
Richard D. James: Producer, performer, remixer
Release date: July 2017
Chart placings: Did not chart
Running time: 18:07
Record label: N/A

The single new project in the avalanche of unreleased Aphex material, *Orphans* was released quietly onto James' website alongside the updates to his other Warp-related projects, which – as we've seen – added bonus tracks sourced from each project's time period. These four also appeared on James' anonymous Soundcloud page as part of the notorious *dump* that housed a whole host of rare tracks.

'Spiral Staircase' was created as a submission to *Future Music* magazine's remix competition in 2004 under the pseudonym Tahnaiya Russell, which challenged entrants to use elements from Luke Vibert's 'Sci-Fi Staircase'. James won the competition, giving the prize to the runner-up, because – as he wrote in the song's Soundcloud bio – 'I had an advantage: knew better than most what Luke liked'.

'Spiral Staircase (Future Music Competition, AFX remix)' (James, Luke Vibert) (5:05)

The first of the two Luke Vibert remixes also comfortably stands as the greatest remix James has released. The skyrocketing arpeggios of the original cultivate a supremely entrancing mood by deepening the array of different time signatures flying through the piece. Also of note is the rhythmic displacement created by the scratchy acid loops, adding an extra 16th note to each bar, to heighten the music's imbalance and entanglement. Moreover, the titanic bass segments and hallucinatory floes of fuzzy pads go even further to enhance the lysergic rapture the production undertakes. Truly magnificent.

'Spiral Staircase (Future Music Competition) (AFX ALTremix b)' (James, Vibert) (4:11)

Picking up where the previous remix left off, the 'ALTremix b' version is less stunning by virtue of its secondary appearance but retains many of the elements to extend the mesmerising electronic display for an extra four minutes. It sounds like James was still working out the best way to include the unique rhythmic features and balance the mix. This version sounds less polished than the take that was eventually used.

'Nightmail 1' (5:02)

This makes use of a sample from John Grierson's reading of the W. H. Auden poem of the same name, with James embedding it firmly into the sprinting acoustic drum loops and spooked 303. Getting into much detail in regard to the instrumentation wouldn't yield many results. However, the ingenious sample-editing and rip-roaring speed cover up any melodic discrepancies.

'4x Atlantis take1' (3:49)

Consisting solely of meaty chunks of marshmallow-like synth, '4x Atlantis...' relies on the innate ear that James has for multifaceted grooves. Wrangling with the limited gear setup, he moulds a liquid deluge of bass timbres and overflowing arpeggios that are left to naturally mingle as they're filtered from behind the scenes. But it still cries out for a trademark Aphex beat to contextualise many of its rhythmic indications.

Collapse (2018)
Alias: Aphex Twin

Personnel:
Richard D. James: Producer, performer
Beau Thomas: Mastering
Release date: September 2018
Chart placings: UK: 11, US: 113
Running time: 28:52 (Original); 35:30 (Website)
Record label: Warp Records

Despite having kept busy with various live performances and the opening of select parts of his mythical archive of unreleased songs, James hadn't released a main Aphex Twin project for two years by the time *Collapse* was announced. Therefore, anticipation ran high when graphics depicting the Aphex Twin logo, stylised in a staggered 3D manner, were discovered in Elephant and Castle station. This oblique tease was followed by similar artworks being placed across the globe in places as distant from one another as Tokyo and New York.

Warp seemingly confirmed the rumours of new music from James in a typically-cryptic press release where the words 'Collapse EP' and parts of the song titles could be found amongst a mix of Cornish language, numbers and plain gibberish. On 7 August, the EP's first single, 'T69 collapse' was released on the Aphex Twin YouTube channel, along with a video by visual artist Weirdcore, who'd been helping James with his innovative live graphics that allowed the audience to manipulate images that appeared on-screen. The video, riffed off the EP's cover, with the Aphex logo stamped into different Cornish locations using 3D scanning and algorithmic AI technology to generate altered images based on the warped styling that could also be seen on the EP's promo images.

The EP was roundly praised, garnering a much better response than the divisive *Computer Controlled Acoustic Instruments* and *Cheetah* projects. Much of the positive criticism stemmed from James' continued percussive skill and knack for complexity, plus the more forward-thinking sound which was compared to *Syro*. Adding to this, James' UK chart run continued – the EP charting just outside the top 10. In the US, it fared much worse, but a spot close to the top 100 is nothing to be sneezed at.

This is the most recent mainline Aphex Twin release, and though there have been multiple unreleased tracks played during live sets and put onto Soundcloud, there's been no word of a follow-up.

'T69 collapse' (5:22)

Broken into a clearly-delineated three-part structure, the first third of 'T69 collapse' hurls out untameable kick drum runs and quaint (in comparison) synth leads that traverse different octaves with ease. But suddenly, this enthralling musical comfort is torn away in a barrage of drum programming that stutters and hammers away at the spooked, glitchy arpeggios. James allows us to climb out of this frightening environment in the last segment, where the gaping leads resurface along with a full-blooded strain of bass jitters. It's purely enchanting: as all the best Aphex tracks are.

'1st 44' (6:09)

Riding the crest of a sub-bass furnished with dizzying circuits of claps and tom-toms, this track feels like a trail of musical dominoes. Every minute detail is set off by a trail of similar studious elements, constantly in danger of falling apart. Whether it's the zippy sound effects, the dolorous curtains of ambient material or the charged-up 360° percussive lattice, James ensures everything works in synergetic harmony.

'MT1 t29r2' (6:04)

This is all about James' unbridled grasp on intoxicating dark hooks. The dichotomy of the child vocals and nursery-rhyme keyboards against the pulverising clangour of the bass and stammering near-atonal raver riff is a tried-and-tested Aphex formula. Nevertheless, he breathes new life into it by juxtaposing galvanising and patently-catchy sections with parts that force the listener to unearth the melodies from the mesh of shifting textures above.

'abundance10edit(2 R8's, FZ20m & a 909)' (6:20)

For the most part, this is the EP's softest track. Morose synths take pride of place, filling in an ominous melody in the first half, before a triumphant one regains control in the latter moments. The bass matches this by darting through a jagged patch until settling on a soapy, slippery mode of playing as the track lurches into its less-hurried portion. It may be the least cohesive piece here, but it still has a myriad of ideas.

'pthex' (4:57)

Commencing with deceptively-chirpy interplay between two weightless synths, 'pthex' rounds off the EP in fine style. The 303 takes up a large chunk of the mix, alternating between background propellor and an up-front driving force. Though the piece has fewer grand changes, the more-subtle shifts – like the gradual unsettling of the melodic parts or the gating effects slicing the whole track apart – prevent it from becoming generic.

Website bonus track
't69 collapse (durichroma)' (6:38)

This is ostensibly an early version of 'T69 collapse' that was left to sprawl out a little more than its judiciously-edited EP counterpart. A bridging section can be found deep into the track with a beautiful solo-lullaby rendition of the chord progression. This is great if you're craving an extended version, but there's little different from the final cut.

London 14.09.2019 (2019)
Alias: Aphex Twin

Personnel:
Richard D. James: Producer, performer
Release date: September 2019
Chart placings: Did not chart
Running time: 20:53
Record label: Warp Records

Another exclusive 12", this time sold at James' outstanding Printworks gig in September 2019. Containing three of the four *Orphans* tracks (in their physical-media debut), unlike the subsequent *Manchester 20.09.2019* EP (which I won't be covering since all its tracks were *Orphaned Deejay Selek* bonuses), there's a brand-new track: 'Soundlab20'. It was released on the Aphex Twin website on 27 December 2019.

'Soundlab20' (6:57)

'Soundlab20' feels like a summation of James' various dabblings in the 2010s. Armed with the elegant sound palette of *Cheetah* and the progressive tendencies of tracks like 'CIRCLONT6A', the track burrows through plateaus of analogue keys, with swells of 303 when the moment demands it. There's also a healthy dose of drum trickery weaving around the gorgeous descending motifs courtesy of some inflated synth tones. Its consignment to being such a rare item doesn't reflect its value as a superb track and a bookend to a prolific James decade.

Peel Session 2 (2019)
Alias: Aphex Twin

Personnel:
Richard D. James: Producer, performer
Release date: November 2019
Original recording date: April 1995
Chart placings: Did not chart
Running time: 21:11
Record label: Warp Records

As part of their 30th-anniversary celebrations, Warp issued a series of archival releases from some of their most famous and defining artists – including Boards of Canada, Flying Lotus and, of course, Aphex Twin. *Peel Session 2* is a recording of James' second John Peel radio session that – contrary to tradition where artists would perform live or semi-live at Maida Vale Studios – was posted to the latter on a DAT tape.

At the time of recording, all versions of the tracks performed here were unreleased. But two of the tracks ('Slo Bird Whistle' and 'p-String') were initially included as part of the 2015 Soundcloud dump. The release of this EP denotes the last *proper* Aphex Twin release – after *Collapse*, which was the most-recent official original project.

'Slo Bird Whistle' (3:33)

Set apart by the incessant bird whistle on the left side, the EP's premiere track is a solid, laid-back slice of IDM. Though the flat drum sound leaves a lot to be desired, the ascending, staccato piano chords and the web of glitchy video-game synths hit a point of nostalgia to adequately compensate for it.

'Radiator (Original Mix)' (6:30)

The so-called 'Original Mix' of the *SAW Volume II* track (the first time a song from that LP has been given an official title (besides 'Blue Calx')) is markedly weaker than the final album version. This is down to the incessant industrial grind of the percussion sucking all the atmosphere out of the familiar woozy bells, leaving the final product curiously inert.

'p-String' (7:02)

This rare track – presumably from the *ICBYD* sessions – bears a lot of the compositional hallmarks of that period – the classical influence on the main melodies, represented by the watery blend of strings and their semitone-separated motifs, and the rough, cacophonous drums, here annoyingly diluted to become little more than a baseline techno slog. Dragged out over seven minutes, it's fortuitous that it never made it to the album.

'Pancake Lizard' (4:06)

To round things out, is a live (though how much is debatable) version of one of the many highlights of the *Donkey Rhubarb* EP. This would've been the track's flagship outing: potentially explaining why it cleaves so close to the EP take. As such, while the quality remains intact, this version is extremely disposable.

Bibliography and sources

General sources
aphextwin.warp.net
Aphex Twin official YouTube channel
rateyourmusic.com
Various sleeve notes and credits
User18081971's Soundcloud page
Analogue Bubblebath

Shirley, I., *Value Added Facts – Mark Darby* (recordcollectormag.com, March 2018)

Digeridoo
Smith, A., *Aphex Twin: Double Trouble* (Melody Maker, May 1992)
Reynolds, S., *Energy Flash: A Journey Through Rave Music and Dance Culture* (Faber & Faber revised edition, 2013)

Xylem Tube
Instagram, @number3_ post (instagram.com, February 2017)
Selected Ambient Works 85-92
Smith, A., *Aphex Twin: Double Trouble* (Melody Maker, May 1992)
Savage, J., *Machine Soul: A History of Techno* (The Village Voice, Summer 1993)

Joyrex J4 & J5
Discogs, *Joyrex J4* listing – https://www.discogs.com/master/19857-Caustic-Window-Joyrex-J4-EP
Discogs, *Joyrex J5* listing – https://www.discogs.com/master/19860-Caustic-Window-Joyrex-J5-EP

Analogue Bubblebath Vol. 3
Discogs, *Analogue Bubblebath Vol. 3* listing – https://www.discogs.com/master/919-AFX-Analogue-Bubblebath-Vol-3
Surfing on Sine Waves
Snapes, L., *The Wheal Thing: Aphex Twin's Alternative Cornish Language* (thequietus.com, September 2016)

Quoth
Discogs, *Quoth* listing – https://www.discogs.com/release/24349-Polygon-Window-Quoth
Joyrex J9i & Joyrex J9ii
Reynolds, S., *Aphex Twin* (Melody Maker, November 1993)
Discogs, *Joyrex J9i* listing – https://www.discogs.com/release/19315-Caustic-Window-Joyrex-J9
Discogs, *Joyrex J9ii* listing – https://www.discogs.com/release/19398-The-Caustic-Window-Joyrex-J9-EP

On
IAmUter, *Aphex Twin – MTV News Feature, 1993* (YouTube, September 2020)
Bradley's Robot:

Discogs, *Bradley's Robot* listing – https://www.discogs.com/release/12276-Strider-B-Bradleys-Robot

Selected Ambient Works, Volume II

Reynolds, S., *Aphex Twin* (Melody Maker, November 1993)

Discogs, *Selected Ambient Works, Volume II* listing – https://www.discogs.com/release/704310-Aphex-Twin-Selected-Ambient-Works-Volume-II

Unidentified author(s), *The SAW II Graphical F.A.Q.* (aphextwin.nu, undated)

Christgau, R., *Consumer Guide: Selected Ambient Works, Volume II* (The Village Voice, May 1994)

Reynolds, S., *Aphex Twin: Selected Ambient Works, Volume II* review (Spin, March 1994)

James, R., *Selected Ambient Works Volume II* bio (aphextwin.warp.net, 2017)

Classics

Cartwright, M., *Aphex Twin: 1995-05-25 Cyberradio VPRO Interview* (YouTube, April 2022)

Discogs, *Classics (Limited Edition, Aqua Blue, Gatefold)* listing – https://www.discogs.com/release/62679-The-Aphex-Twin-Classics

Discogs, *We Have Arrived (Remixes By Aphex Twin & The Mover)* listing – https://www.discogs.com/master/6696-Mescalinum-United-We-Have-Arrived-Remixes-By-Aphex-Twin-The-Mover

...I Care Because You Do

Red Bull Music Academy, *Philip Glass on His Collaboration With Aphex Twin | Red Bull Music Academy* (YouTube, February 2019)

Prince, D., *...I Care Because You Do* review (Rolling Stone, May 1995)

Browne, D., *...I Care Because You Do* review (Entertainment Weekly, June 1995)

Donkey Rhubarb

Red Bull Music Academy, *Philip Glass on His Collaboration With Aphex Twin | Red Bull Music Academy* (YouTube, February 2019)

Bradley's Beat

Press release, *Brad Strider – Bradley's Beat* (RTM Distribution, September 1995)

Expert Knob Twiddlers

Gross, J., *µ-Zic Interview by James Gross* (Perfect Sound Forever, September 1997)

Bulut, S., *The 20 tracks that define Planet Mu, according to Mike Paradinas* (Dummy, September 2015)

Richard D. James Album

Gross, J., *Aphex Twin* (Perfect Sound Forever, September 1997)

Thompson, B., *The Aphex Twin* (Seven Years of Plenty, 1998)

Hermes, W., *Aphex Twin: Richard D. James Album* review (Spin, February 1997)

Thomas, B., *120 essential pop albums* (The Telegraph, January 2008)

Girl/Boy

Jones, R., *Is the Aphex Twin completely mad?* (Jockey Slut, October/November 1996)

Come to Daddy

Discogs, *Come to Daddy Remixed* listing – https://www.discogs.com/release/28701-Aphex-Twin-Come-To-Daddy-Remixed

phresch, *Aphex Twin – Come to Daddy (Live Version) HD* (YouTube, February 2011)

Windowlicker

"The Windowlickers" – artwork created by H.R. Giger (1999)

Kahney, L., *Hey, Who's That Face in My Song?* (Wired, May 2002)

Niimo, J., *The Aphex Face* (bastwood.com, unknown date)

James, R., *Windowlicker* bio (aphextwin.warp.net, 2017)

Drukqs

Hoffmann, H., *Aphex Twin Interview* (Groove, 2001)

Litterest, G., *The History of the Disklavier, Part 1* (hub.yamaha.com, 2017)

James, R., *Diskbat ALL prepared1mix (snr2mix)* bio (soundcloud.com, 2015)

Michaels, J., *Aphex Twin: Kanye tried to get away with not paying for Avril 14th sample* (The Guardian, August 2014)

AFX / LFO

Discogs, *AFX / LFO* listing – https://www.discogs.com/release/494794-LFO-AFX-Untitled

Confederation Trough

Pattison, L., *Dancing in the Dark* (The Guardian, May 2007)

Discogs, *Aphex Mt. Fuji 2017* listing – https://www.discogs.com/release/10631286-Aphex-Twin-Aphex-Mt-Fuji-2017

Caustic Window

Unidentified author(s), *Aphex Twin's unreleased Caustic Window album is now available digitally through Kickstarter* (Fact, April 2014)

Syro

Minsker, E., *An Aphex Twin Blimp Is Flying Over London | News* (Pitchfork, August 2014)

Minsker, E., *Aphex Twin announces new album Syro Via the Deep Web* (Pitchfork, August 2014)

Sherburne, P., *Strange Visitor: A Conversation with Aphex Twin* (Pitchfork, September 2014)

NTS, *Aphex Twin live at Barbican Hall, London, 10/10/12* (YouTube, June 2019)

James, R., *Syro* bio (aphextwin.warp.net, 2017)

Computer Controlled Acoustic Instruments pt2

Beaumont-Thomas, B., *Aphex Twin – Computer Controlled Acoustic Instruments pt2 review: "Sometimes unlistenably irritating"* (The Guardian, January 2015)

Richardson, M., *Aphex Twin – Computer Controlled Acoustic Instruments pt2 EP/Album Reviews* (Pitchfork, January 2015)

Cheetah

Diego (last name unknown), *Aphex Twin's Cheetah at Summer NAMM* (Zzounds, June 2016)

Unknown author(s), *Cheetah EP – New Product Information* (cheetah-ep.com, June 2016)

Houston, T.X. 12.17.16

Discogs, *Houston, T.X. 12.17.16* listing – https://www.discogs.com/master/1523549-AFX-Houston-TX-121716

London 03.06.17

NTS, *Aphex Twin Live at Field Day 2017 (alt. audio)* (YouTube, June 2017)

Discogs, *London 03.06.17* listing – https://www.discogs.com/master/1212065-AFX-London-030617

Korg Trax+Tunings for falling asleep

James, R., *Richard D. James speaks to Tatsuya Takahashi* (Warp, July 2017)

James, R., *Korg Trax+Tunings for falling asleep* bio (aphextwin.warp.net, July 2017)

Orphans

Discogs, *Luke Vibert Spiral Staircase (Future Music Competition) (AFX Remix)* listing – https://www.discogs.com/release/6612574-user48736353001-Luke-Vibert-Spiral-Staircase-Future-Music-Competition-AFX-Remix

Collapse

Snapes, L., *Mystery images at tube station hint at new Aphex Twin album* (The Guardian, July 2018)

Warp Records tweet (Twitter, August 2018)

London 14.09.2019

Discogs, *London 14.09.2019* listing – https://www.discogs.com/master/1658714-Aphex-Twin-London-14092019

Peel Session 2

Warp, *Releases – Aphex Twin – Peel Session 2* (warp.net, November 2019)

On Track series
Alan Parsons Project – Steve Swift 978-1-78952-154-2
Tori Amos – Lisa Torem 978-1-78952-142-9
Asia – Peter Braidis 978-1-78952-099-6
Badfinger – Robert Day-Webb 978-1-878952-176-4
Barclay James Harvest – Keith and Monica Domone 978-1-78952-067-5
The Beatles – Andrew Wild 978-1-78952-009-5
The Beatles Solo 1969-1980 – Andrew Wild 978-1-78952-030-9
Blue Oyster Cult – Jacob Holm-Lupo 978-1-78952-007-1
Blur – Matt Bishop – 978-178952-164-1
Marc Bolan and T.Rex – Peter Gallagher 978-1-78952-124-5
Kate Bush – Bill Thomas 978-1-78952-097-2
Camel – Hamish Kuzminski 978-1-78952-040-8
Caravan – Andy Boot 978-1-78952-127-6
Cardiacs – Eric Benac 978-1-78952-131-3
Eric Clapton Solo – Andrew Wild 978-1-78952-141-2
The Clash – Nick Assirati 978-1-78952-077-4
Crosby, Stills and Nash – Andrew Wild 978-1-78952-039-2
The Damned – Morgan Brown 978-1-78952-136-8
Deep Purple and Rainbow 1968-79 – Steve Pilkington 978-1-78952-002-6
Dire Straits – Andrew Wild 978-1-78952-044-6
The Doors – Tony Thompson 978-1-78952-137-5
Dream Theater – Jordan Blum 978-1-78952-050-7
Electric Light Orchestra – Barry Delve 978-1-78952-152-8
Elvis Costello and The Attractions – Georg Purvis 978-1-78952-129-0
Emerson Lake and Palmer – Mike Goode 978-1-78952-000-2
Fairport Convention – Kevan Furbank 978-1-78952-051-4
Peter Gabriel – Graeme Scarfe 978-1-78952-138-2
Genesis – Stuart MacFarlane 978-1-78952-005-7
Gentle Giant – Gary Steel 978-1-78952-058-3
Gong – Kevan Furbank 978-1-78952-082-8
Hall and Oates – Ian Abrahams 978-1-78952-167-2
Hawkwind – Duncan Harris 978-1-78952-052-1
Peter Hammill – Richard Rees Jones 978-1-78952-163-4
Roy Harper – Opher Goodwin 978-1-78952-130-6
Jimi Hendrix – Emma Stott 978-1-78952-175-7
The Hollies – Andrew Darlington 978-1-78952-159-7
Iron Maiden – Steve Pilkington 978-1-78952-061-3
Jefferson Airplane – Richard Butterworth 978-1-78952-143-6
Jethro Tull – Jordan Blum 978-1-78952-016-3
Elton John in the 1970s – Peter Kearns 978-1-78952-034-7
The Incredible String Band – Tim Moon 978-1-78952-107-8
Iron Maiden – Steve Pilkington 978-1-78952-061-3
Judas Priest – John Tucker 978-1-78952-018-7
Kansas – Kevin Cummings 978-1-78952-057-6
The Kinks – Martin Hutchinson 978-1-78952-172-6
Korn – Matt Karpe 978-1-78952-153-5
Led Zeppelin – Steve Pilkington 978-1-78952-151-1
Level 42 – Matt Philips 978-1-78952-102-3

Little Feat – 978-1-78952-168-9
Aimee Mann – Jez Rowden 978-1-78952-036-1
Joni Mitchell – Peter Kearns 978-1-78952-081-1
The Moody Blues – Geoffrey Feakes 978-1-78952-042-2
Motorhead – Duncan Harris 978-1-78952-173-3
Mike Oldfield – Ryan Yard 978-1-78952-060-6
Opeth – Jordan Blum 978-1-78-952-166-5
Tom Petty – Richard James 978-1-78952-128-3
Porcupine Tree – Nick Holmes 978-1-78952-144-3
Queen – Andrew Wild 978-1-78952-003-3
Radiohead – William Allen 978-1-78952-149-8
Renaissance – David Detmer 978-1-78952-062-0
The Rolling Stones 1963-80 – Steve Pilkington 978-1-78952-017-0
The Smiths and Morrissey – Tommy Gunnarsson 978-1-78952-140-5
Status Quo the Frantic Four Years – Richard James 978-1-78952-160-3
Steely Dan – Jez Rowden 978-1-78952-043-9
Steve Hackett – Geoffrey Feakes 978-1-78952-098-9
Thin Lizzy – Graeme Stroud 978-1-78952-064-4
Toto – Jacob Holm-Lupo 978-1-78952-019-4
U2 – Eoghan Lyng 978-1-78952-078-1
UFO – Richard James 978-1-78952-073-6
The Who – Geoffrey Feakes 978-1-78952-076-7
Roy Wood and the Move – James R Turner 978-1-78952-008-8
Van Der Graaf Generator – Dan Coffey 978-1-78952-031-6
Yes – Stephen Lambe 978-1-78952-001-9
Frank Zappa 1966 to 1979 – Eric Benac 978-1-78952-033-0
Warren Zevon – Peter Gallagher 978-1-78952-170-2
10CC – Peter Kearns 978-1-78952-054-5

Decades Series

The Bee Gees in the 1960s – Andrew Môn Hughes et al 978-1-78952-148-1
The Bee Gees in the 1970s – Andrew Môn Hughes et al 978-1-78952-179-5
Black Sabbath in the 1970s – Chris Sutton 978-1-78952-171-9
Britpop – Peter Richard Adams and Matt Pooler 978-1-78952-169-6
Alice Cooper in the 1970s – Chris Sutton 978-1-78952-104-7
Curved Air in the 1970s – Laura Shenton 978-1-78952-069-9
Bob Dylan in the 1980s – Don Klees 978-1-78952-157-3
Fleetwood Mac in the 1970s – Andrew Wild 978-1-78952-105-4
Focus in the 1970s – Stephen Lambe 978-1-78952-079-8
Free and Bad Company in the 1970s – John Van der Kiste 978-1-78952-178-8
Genesis in the 1970s – Bill Thomas 978178952-146-7
George Harrison in the 1970s – Eoghan Lyng 978-1-78952-174-0
Marillion in the 1980s – Nathaniel Webb 978-1-78952-065-1
Mott the Hoople and Ian Hunter in the 1970s – John Van der Kiste
978-1-78-952-162-7
Pink Floyd In The 1970s – Georg Purvis 978-1-78952-072-9
Tangerine Dream in the 1970s – Stephen Palmer 978-1-78952-161-0
The Sweet in the 1970s – Darren Johnson from Gary Cosby collection 978-1-78952-
139-9

Uriah Heep in the 1970s – Steve Pilkington 978-1-78952-103-0
Yes in the 1980s – Stephen Lambe with David Watkinson 978-1-78952-125-2

On Screen series
Carry On... – Stephen Lambe 978-1-78952-004-0
David Cronenberg – Patrick Chapman 978-1-78952-071-2
Doctor Who: The David Tennant Years – Jamie Hailstone 978-1-78952-066-8
James Bond – Andrew Wild – 978-1-78952-010-1
Monty Python – Steve Pilkington 978-1-78952-047-7
Seinfeld Seasons 1 to 5 – Stephen Lambe 978-1-78952-012-5

Other Books
1967: A Year In Psychedelic Rock – Kevan Furbank 978-1-78952-155-9
1970: A Year In Rock – John Van der Kiste 978-1-78952-147-4
1973: The Golden Year of Progressive Rock 978-1-78952-165-8
Babysitting A Band On The Rocks – G.D. Praetorius 978-1-78952-106-1
Eric Clapton Sessions – Andrew Wild 978-1-78952-177-1
Derek Taylor: For Your Radioactive Children – Andrew Darlington
978-1-78952-038-5
The Golden Road: The Recording History of The Grateful Dead – John Kilbride 978-1-
78952-156-6
Iggy and The Stooges On Stage 1967-1974 – Per Nilsen 978-1-78952-101-6
Jon Anderson and the Warriors – the road to Yes – David Watkinson
978-1-78952-059-0
Nu Metal: A Definitive Guide – Matt Karpe 978-1-78952-063-7
Tommy Bolin: In and Out of Deep Purple – Laura Shenton 978-1-78952-070-5
Maximum Darkness – Deke Leonard 978-1-78952-048-4
Maybe I Should've Stayed In Bed – Deke Leonard 978-1-78952-053-8
The Twang Dynasty – Deke Leonard 978-1-78952-049-1

and many more to come!

Would you like to write for Sonicbond Publishing?

At Sonicbond Publishing we are always on the look-out for authors, particularly for our two main series:

On Track. Mixing fact with in depth analysis, the On Track series examines the work of a particular musical artist or group. All genres are considered from easy listening and jazz to 60s soul to 90s pop, via rock and metal.

On Screen. This series looks at the world of film and television. Subjects considered include directors, actors and writers, as well as entire television and film series. As with the On Track series, we balance fact with analysis.

While professional writing experience would, of course, be an advantage the most important qualification is to have real enthusiasm and knowledge of your subject. First-time authors are welcomed, but the ability to write well in English is essential.

Sonicbond Publishing has distribution throughout Europe and North America, and all books are also published in E-book form. Authors will be paid a royalty based on sales of their book.

Further details are available from www.sonicbondpublishing.co.uk. To contact us, complete the contact form there or email info@sonicbondpublishing.co.uk